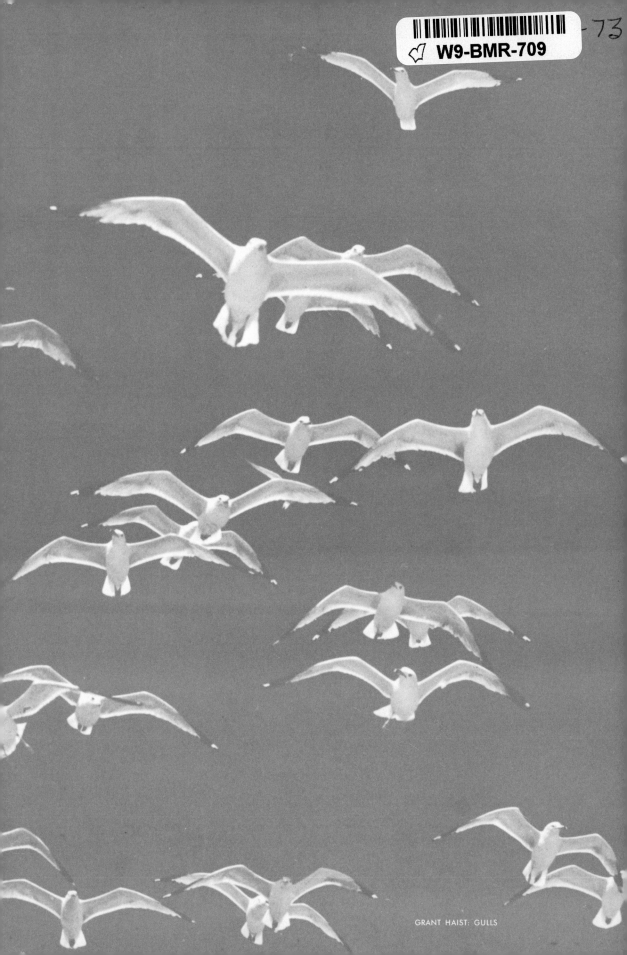

GRANT HAIST: GULLS

OUR LIVING WORLD OF NATURE

The
Life
of the
Seashore

Developed jointly with The World Book Encyclopedia

*Produced with the cooperation of
The United States Department of the Interior*

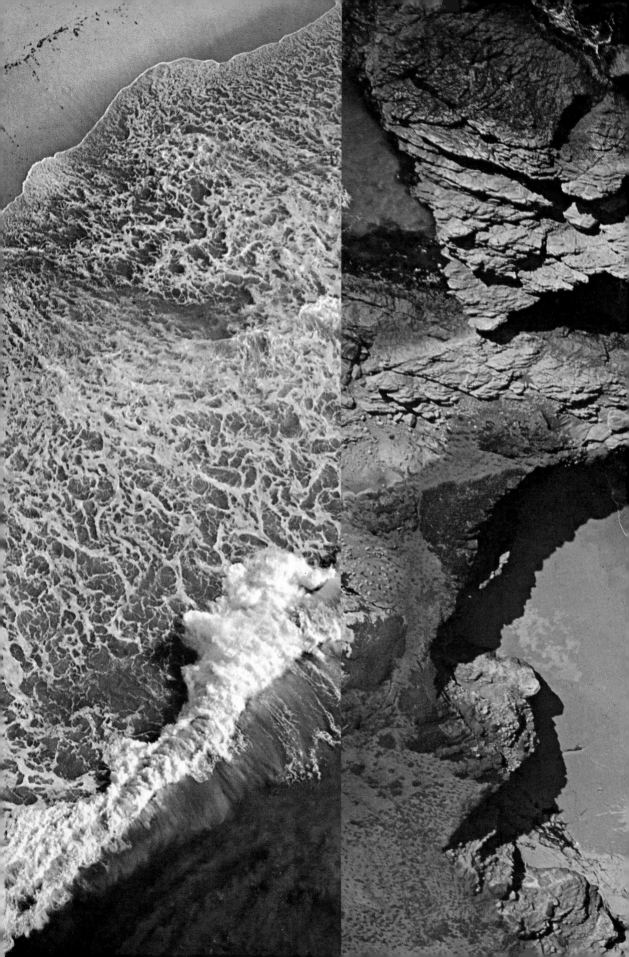

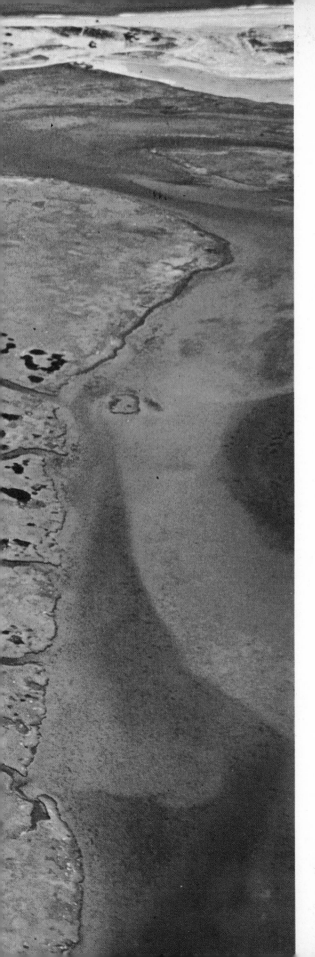

OUR LIVING WORLD OF NATURE

The
Life
of the
Seashore

WILLIAM H. AMOS

Published in cooperation with
The World Book Encyclopedia

McGraw-Hill Book Company
NEW YORK   TORONTO   LONDON

WILLIAM H. AMOS *was raised in the Orient, where he first was introduced to marine life along the shores of the Philippine Islands and the Inland Sea of Japan. Mr. Amos has been associated with the New York Zoological Society and with a number of marine laboratories in the United States and abroad, and he was a member of the Smithsonian–Bredin Expedition to the Lesser Antilles a few years ago. He is Chairman of the Science Department of St. Andrew's School in Middletown, Delaware, and he is a Research Associate of the University of Delaware Marine Laboratory and a Senior Visiting Investigator at the Systematics–Ecology Program at the Marine Biological Laboratory in Woods Hole, Massachusetts, where he also serves as a consultant in biophotography. Mr. Amos's major interests are both fresh-water and marine organisms, particularly those of coastal estuaries. He is the author of many articles and books on marine and aquatic biology, most of which have been illustrated with his own biophotographs.*

Library of Congress Catalog Card Number: 66–17515

0 NR 72

ISBN 07-046004-3

OUR LIVING WORLD OF NATURE

Science Editor

RICHARD B. FISCHER   *Cornell University*

Board of Consultants

ROLAND CLEMENT   *National Audubon Society*

C. GORDON FREDINE   *National Park Service, The United States Department of the Interior*

WILLIAM H. NAULT   *Field Enterprises Educational Corporation*

BENJAMIN NICHOLS   *Cornell University*

EUGENE P. ODUM   *University of Georgia*

HENRY J. OOSTING   *Duke University*

OLIN SEWALL PETTINGILL, JR.   *Cornell University*

DAVID PIMENTEL   *Cornell University*

PAUL B. SEARS   *Yale University*

ROBERT L. USINGER   *University of California*

Readability Consultant

JOSEPHINE PIEKARZ IVES   *New York University*

Special Consultants for The Life of the Seashore

MELBOURNE R. CARRIKER   *Marine Biological Laboratory, Woods Hole, Massachusetts*

RALPH W. DEXTER   *Kent State University*

Contents

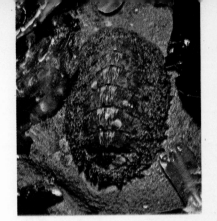

Rhythms of the Sea

The sea at last! You may have traveled a thousand miles to get here, or perhaps you have only stepped across the road. Whatever the journey required, to those who love the sea it is always thrilling to stand at its edge.

You are on a rocky point overlooking the waters of another world. The dust, the dry fields, the city streets lie behind; a cool constantly moving surface of changing blues and greens stretches ahead. The smell and feel of the salt air are invigorating.

Below, a parade of waves crowds together, rises high, breaks into foam, and then slams with a mighty roar against the rocks. Far out a few porpoises rise and disappear; gulls wheel and cry overhead. Living creatures inhabit the open sea and ride the winds above it, but what about the shifting sand and battered rocks at its edge? Surely the changes of tides and waves and seasons, the alternating exposure to sun and air, and then to salt water make the shore a difficult place for life.

A quick climb down from your rocky point answers the question. Nearer the water's edge, the rocks are slippery with

Colorful algae survive the ceaseless battering of waves and the unending rise and fall of tide where land meets sea. Hidden among the seaweeds are scores of animals equally well adapted to life in this changeable environment.

small plants called *algae*. Closer to the shoreline are larger and longer algae—the true seaweeds. In the water their brown, red, or green leaflike fronds are whipped back and forth as waves rush up and ebb back into the sea. Obviously these soft plants do survive ceaseless battering.

Hold up a piece of limp seaweed and trace it downward; you will discover a strong cordlike stalk, the base of which spreads out and clings to the surface of a rock. This base is called a *holdfast*. And it does hold fast. Indeed, its only job is to grip the rock firmly. Unlike the true roots of land plants, a holdfast is not a special absorbing organ that takes in substances from the rocky base to which it is attached. The seaweed itself is a simple plant whose fronds absorb minerals from the water, as the roots of more familiar land plants absorb minerals from the water of the soil, and they trap energy from the sun to manufacture their own substance, as green leaves do.

Simple though it is, a seaweed is so beautifully adapted to its difficult habitat that not only does it support itself, it also serves as a place of shelter for other living things. A piece of seaweed plucked from the ocean and swished gently in a shallow pan of water will usually release a number of small, active animals. Some have been clinging with strong curved claws, but others lack such equipment. A few build tubes or other permanent attachments directly onto the plant itself. Watch a seaweed while a wave surges past: the force of water is diminished by the tangled forest of algal stalks and fronds. In fact, near the rock water moves so gently that various animals can creep around holdfasts and stalks without being washed away. It is like the quiet of a forest floor when a strong wind tosses the tops of trees high overhead.

Where does the sea get this energy and how do seashore plants and animals withstand it?

The origin of the waves

It all begins as the sun's heat generates currents in the atmosphere. Breezes and winds create friction with the surface of the sea; water absorbs some of the energy of wind and develops waves. You can make miniature waves yourself by blowing across water in a shallow pan; or experiment carefully with an electric fan that has different speeds. The farther wind blows across water, the larger the waves—the strength of wind has less effect on wave height than does the distance over which the wind has blown.

Although the great waves of the open ocean may seem blunt and unhurried, they can travel faster than the wind that generates them. But despite their speed and power,

A thirty-foot fountain of spray bursts through a blowhole at West Maui, Hawaii. Pounding relentlessly at the lava headland, waves probably first eroded a cave in the face of the porous rock, then gnawed a hole through its roof. Each incoming swell now jets upward like a geyser and settles to the rocks in a curtain of mist.

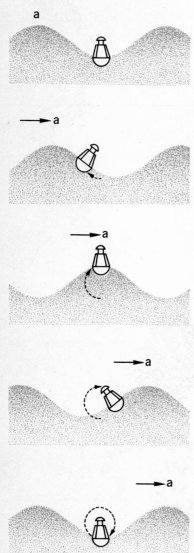

waves do not carry along the water through which they move, except when they are close to shore.

Watch gulls resting on the water several hundred yards out. They stay in one spot, floating up and down as waves run beneath them. The waves do not push them along at all. Why?

Perhaps you have seen waves created by wind in wheatfields. These are genuine waves, yet the stalks of wheat go nowhere. When you whip a rope on the ground, waves ripple along its length, yet the rope remains where it was. A wave is a form of energy that can travel through solids, liquids, and gases, even through empty space. Matter may transmit a wave, but the matter does not have to flow along with it.

Although waves extend below the surface, their effects decrease with depth. Swimmers dive beneath a breaker plunging toward the beach to escape its full impact.

As waves near the shore, they rise and begin to plunge forward in the familiar shape of foaming breakers, or surf. Then the energy from the wind over hundreds—perhaps thousands—of miles of open ocean bursts upon a headland with a force of as much as twenty-five tons a square yard. The water picks up particles of sand, even stones, which scour the shore.

In its attack on the cliff, each wave has been compressed by the rising bottom, and then it does carry along a great deal of water. That is why it is dangerous to dive and swim near rocks, even though you may want to look at the animals and plants there. Swimmers cannot withstand the rush of the water, and bad scrapes or broken bones may result from swimming among rocks on which waves break.

Of course, no cliff is battered by a single, occasional wave, but by a continuous train of them—day and night, year after year, century after century. It is easy to count waves and to discover that, depending to some extent on the slope of the bottom, under normal wind conditions approximately five waves arrive every minute. Hence, a rocky shore and all living things there may suffer a blow every twelve seconds.

As waves enter the shallow water near shore, the rising slope of the bottom forces the water into crests that plunge forward in the form of breakers. Racing up the beach in sheets of foam and washing back into the sea, the water constantly rearranges the sand and reshapes the contours of the coastline.

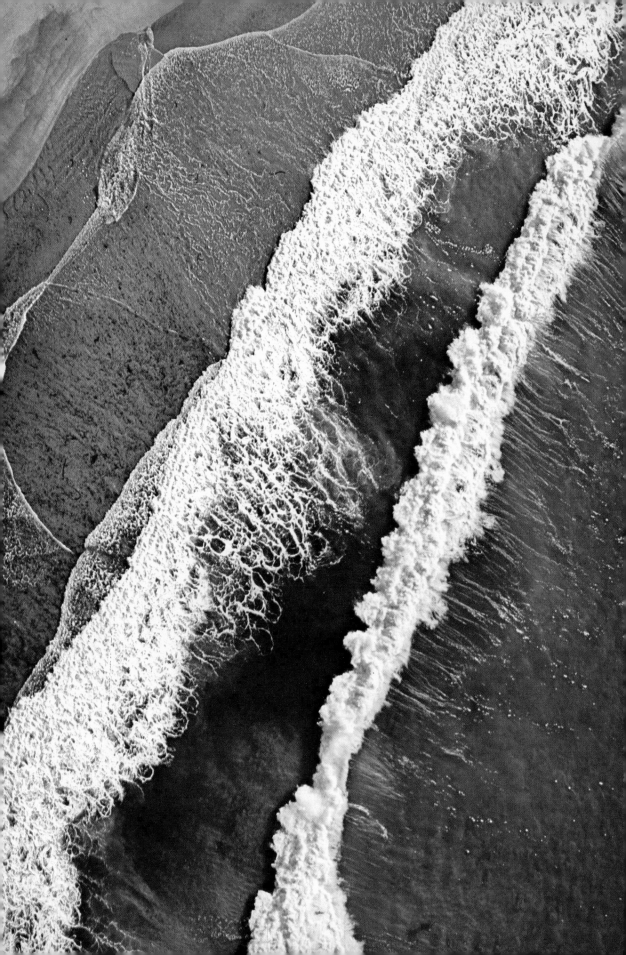

Defense against the waves

Over millions of years, the animals and plants of the sea-shore rocks have evolved many defenses against waves. For example, on the rocks are hundreds of little, cone-shaped shells. These are barnacles, animals common to rocky shores. A barnacle can be crushed easily by the blow of a hammer. Yet in a storm it withstands repeated blows of similar force —some forty pounds on the square inch of rock it occupies.

The barnacle survives not simply through the brute strength of its shell, but rather through its design. The shell is strong and fairly thick; more important, its closely inter-locked limy plates form a cone which presents the waves a small curved surface to act upon. Water splits around it, dividing the force, and the barnacle survives very well. Barnacles close their shells when surf pounds them; then, when the tide comes and water covers them, they extend feathery legs through an opening formed by a pair of movable plates, or *valves*, at the top of the cone and begin to feed by waving these legs and forcing water into their shells. The water contains oxygen as well as microscopic plants and animals that the barnacles eat.

Instead of hardness and toughness, some organisms depend on extreme softness. Seaweeds, such as kelp and sea lettuce, as well as long-branching animal colonies—sea whips,

A flowerlike sea anemone *(above)* defies the waves by clinging firmly to rocks, where its thick muscular body is able to endure the battering of sand-laden water. When the waves become too strong, or when falling tide exposes them to the air, anemones contract into stumplike mounds *(below)* with their delicate feeding tentacles folded inside.

hydroids, and other anchored forms—simply sway back and forth with each wave, streaming out in the water as it rushes by.

In addition to avoiding being smashed by the force of the waves, life on a rocky shore has to keep from being washed away. Here, too, there are several ways of meeting the problem.

Seaweeds have holdfasts. Barnacles and oysters cement themselves firmly in place when they first settle as larvae, never again to move as long as they live. Mussels attach strong anchor lines, known as byssus threads, to the rocks. Sea urchins often wedge themselves firmly into crevices from which waves cannot dislodge them; nor can grasping human hands get them loose without breaking off dozens of sharp, strong spines.

A heavy muscular foot keeps limpets, chitons, and other snails in place. Reach down and try to grasp a limpet. Your fingers slide off the wet cone. Even if you can get your fingernails under the shell, you will have to pull very hard to loosen the animal. The eight-plated chiton uses its large, flat foot to hug the rocks just as strongly. Yet when the tide covers these animals, they glide smoothly over a rock face, obtaining food by rasping off microscopic algae.

Sea stars (starfish), on the other hand, cling to a rock just as powerfully, but, lacking a large muscular foot, use hundreds of tiny, sucking tube feet.

Some of these animals are secure enough to feed as well as to hang on while being battered by waves. A close look reveals that the two shells of mussels and oysters are slightly open in the face of waves, so the animals can draw in water to strain out microscopic organisms. Even barnacles sometimes extend their feathery legs into weaker waves.

Naturally, not all living things are successful all the time. A rock that has broken off a cliff rolls around in the surf, smashing all the barnacles, mussels, and other animals attached to it. Waves do make living among the rocks insecure and often temporary. Yet this has not discouraged life. When a bit of rock breaks off, the newly exposed surface almost immediately begins to be covered by microscopic plants. Gradually others succeed them. How they come to rest long enough to cling still puzzles investigators.

Careful observation along a rocky coast such as that in Acadia National Park, Maine, or in Olympic National Park, Washington, will reveal most of the organisms described

KELP

FROND

HOLDFAST

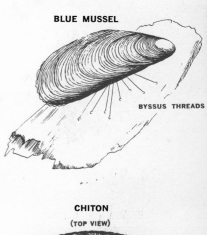

BLUE MUSSEL

BYSSUS THREADS

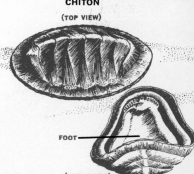

CHITON
(TOP VIEW)

FOOT

(UNDERSIDE)

15

Too small to be seen without magnification, a multitude of tiny animals drifts with currents near the surface of the sea. Widely varied in form, planktonic animals feed on even smaller one-cell plants and are eaten in turn by each other and by a host of larger animals.

here. If they are not exposed at low tide, you may have to peer into the water through a glass-bottom bucket. The first look could disappoint you, because water near the shore is often murky, or turbid, as a result of sand and sediment in it. Perhaps you can see only a few inches. You might want to try lying on a rock and putting your face into the water while wearing a face mask. Another way to get some idea of life in the water close to shore is to make a fine-mesh net of an old handkerchief or pillow case. By sweeping it through the water you can usually capture many things. Rinse them out into a container of sea water. A magnifying glass should reveal small moving animals, which, along with other tiny animals and plants, make up what is called the *plankton* of the ocean. Your catch will also include decayed remains of plants and animals—and sand.

Sandpipers probe the wet sand, searching for mole crabs and other small animals. As the next wave surges in, the sandpipers will scurry up the beach just ahead of the surf.

Dwellers of the sand

Probably the kind of shoreline most people think of first is not a rocky one, where so much life can be seen easily, but the beach. You can find good examples of extensive beaches at Cape Cod, Fire Island, Cape Hatteras, and Padre Island National Seashores. When you go to the beach on a bright summer day, you won't see much in the way of animal life until you discover where and how to look. As you walk across the sand, gulls that had been standing quietly at the water's edge rise into the air, mew noisily, and fly farther down the beach. Probably the only obvious source of living movement that remains is a sandpiper. With twinkling feet these little birds run across the beach toward the water, pausing to probe the wet sand with their long bills. As waves surge in, sandpipers scurry up the slope of the beach, always keeping just out of reach of water. Suddenly they too take to the air and flash to a spot several dozen yards away.

There is nothing else alive near you. Or is there?

The beach certainly seems barren. Some of its animals are sand-colored and blend with the background; others burrow

17

into sand; still others are so small that they live in spaces between sand grains. All reside in distinct zones of a beach between the water and the barrier sand dunes higher up. A beach supports a heavy population indeed, but you have to look hard to find it.

A hunt for one inhabitant and a study of its ways will show you how to find and observe other beach animals. Walk toward the water. Probably you still see only the waves which rush in, soak into the sand, then flood back in great sheets toward the sea, where they join the next incoming wave. Standing with your bare feet awash, you watch this rhythmic ebb and flow until it lulls you into a quiet trance.

Suddenly the sand beneath your feet wiggles and you look down with alarm. The entire beach erupts into countless small oval figures that scurry down the slope, only to disappear as the next wave rolls in. For a while nothing happens. Then, as if at some mysterious signal, hundreds of little shapes rise out of the sand as the water ebbs seaward. They coast down with the water and suddenly sink out of sight just before the next wave crests above them.

Mark the place at which one has disappeared and watch carefully. There may be no sign of life until the water flows gently over the spot on its return trip to the sea. Then you may for a moment see two feathery objects poke up from

the sand, to disappear once more when a new wave rushes in.

Quickly scoop up sand in the area and there, in the wet sand in your hand, you may find a small animal with a shiny, smooth, gray-white body. It digs frantically and nestles against your palm. If you hold it firmly without crushing it and wash the sand away you will find a mole crab, one of the most unusual crustaceans on our shores.

There are two closely related mole crabs in the United States: *Emerita analoga* of the Pacific coast and *Emerita talpoida*, found along the Atlantic coast. Mole crabs do not have the customary flat crab shape; they have longer abdomens like hermit crabs, their relatives that carry around snail shells. These two species of *Emerita* are almost identical. Other, less common kinds of mole crabs are quite different in shape and activity, although they too live in sandy beaches.

Place your captured *Emerita* in a container of sea water with an inch of sand in the bottom. There you can watch it burrow instantly, leaving no trace. You will have to be patient to see exactly how it does so, for this is one of the fastest and most efficient diggers anywhere.

First, examine your captive's body. The jointed abdomen ends in a heavy, triangular tail, or *telson*. The fanlike pad-

Wheeling overhead in noisy flocks or searching the beach for food cast up by the tide, gulls are a familiar sight along every shore. Gulls devour small crustaceans, mussels, clams, dead fish, and almost anything else that is edible.

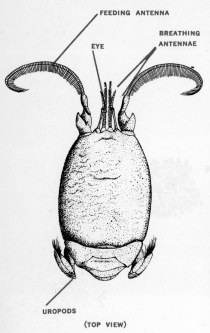

MOLE CRAB

FEEDING ANTENNA

EYE

BREATHING
ANTENNAE

UROPODS

(TOP VIEW)

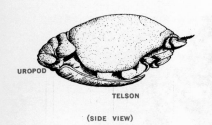

UROPOD

TELSON

(SIDE VIEW)

dles on each side are known as *uropods*; powerful muscles run from the abdomen and telson into these paddles. Watch through the sides of a glass container in which you have a mole crab in sea water but no sand, and you will see the uropods sculling as rapidly as tiny propellers. In the sand this movement quickly excavates a hole and throws sand grains up on top of the crab. At the same time several pairs of legs push sand forward and to the side, so that the entire animal seems almost to melt into the sand in a split second. The oval, streamlined shape of the mole crab helps it push itself into the sand.

Once under, the crab must keep its gills, or breathing organs, clean and free of sand grains. It does this with a special pair of legs that comb sand out of the gills. The gills take oxygen from the water that comes to the crab. To get rid of water, the little creature presses together four long filaments of its first pair of feelers (or *antennae*) to form an exit canal through which it exhales used water in a miniature jet stream.

After settling deeply into sand, the mole crab anchors itself with its telson. Then it extends a pair of minute eyes on long, jointed stalks above the sand to see what is going on.

While you usually do not notice a mole crab in the beach, it may by chance signal its presence as vividly as if it had waved a flag. The "flag" is bright green, and the crab, which is seeking to hide, has nothing to do with waving it.

One of the most common shore plants is a green seaweed, *Ulva,* known as sea lettuce. *Ulva* lives best in the zone covered by tides, wherever there are rocks and other firm surfaces to cling to. Naturally, on a shifting, sandy beach, there are few of these other than occasional pebbles. Occasionally a spore of *Ulva* will settle on the one part of *Emerita* that is normally exposed: the tips of the first antennae that form the breathing tube. As you walk along a beach, watch for an occasional streamer of sea lettuce. Scoop it up to discover where it is attached. Most often you will find a pebble, but once in a while the prize at the end of the green strand will be a fat mole crab.

Several fronds of sea lettuce stream like pennants from the tip of a mole crab's two-branched antenna. When the inch-long crustacean burrows backward into the sand, the four branches of these two antennae are pressed together to form a breathing tube which projects slightly from the sand.

Feeders in the surf

The waves naturally bring in large quantities of tiny floating, drifting plants and animals, known as *plankton,* to the beach. Many animals there live off this rich source of food, but none is more efficient at harvesting it than the mole crab.

Place a mole crab in sand in a large container of sea water, such as a dishpan or an aquarium, and rock it. This will cause small waves to wash from one end to the other over the buried animal. As soon as your waves surge overhead, the crab should unfurl another pair of antennae. Long and feathery, each one has as many as 150 joints. A thousand or more tiny hairs on each second antenna form an efficient sieve that strains from water a never-ending supply of minute planktonic plants and animals. The sieves are so fine they may even be able to trap bacteria.

Because its jaws are very weak, the mole crab eats its food whole. It neatly rolls up each antenna, one at a time, and brings it down close to the mouth. Specialized mouth parts then scrape food from the hairs and fringes.

This little crab must always stay in the path of plankton-bearing waves. Since tides on most shores flood and ebb twice daily, the water line changes constantly. A mole crab feeds in one spot until, by delicate senses we hardly appreciate, it feels a change in the wave pressure. During flood tide it moves up the beach, during ebb tide it follows the water

Delicate fringes of fine bristles on a mole crab's feeding antennae strain plankton from the water as backwash rushes down the beach. Its eyes, each at the tip of a long, jointed stalk, are visible on either side of the breathing antennae.

down. It always burrows backward into the sand, facing the water, and lies at an angle of about 45 degrees to the sand surface. It feeds only when water runs down the beach, not while waves roll in.

This little shell-encased creature is remarkably sensitive to things that tell it where it is and what conditions are. For instance, if you allow one to dig in moist sand away from waves but slosh a bucketful of water across the sand over its head, it will immediately face into the "current." If you place it in a dish of wet sand and hold up a piece of black paper or dark cloth at one side, it will turn toward the dark place. Why? Look around you: the beach is glaring white, the water dark blue; mole crabs always face dark water.

No one really knows how much plankton the millions of mole crabs on our shores remove from water, but surely they play an important part in controlling the numbers of plants and animals there. It is true, however, that they also release their young into the water, adding to the plankton. But whether they act as cannibals, no one knows. Even if they do, most of their young would still be swept out to sea.

Mole crabs serve as an important food for larger animals. Since they cannot defend themselves, and can only hide in the sand, they are hunted by many predators—including swimming crabs, certain fish, and birds. Sandpipers probe for mole crabs, which they apparently find with ease. Perhaps these sharp-eyed birds see jets of water exhaled by the crabs.

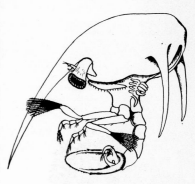

Shown here nearly fifty times its actual size, a mole crab zoea looks far different from the adult animal. The minute, free-swimming zoea larvae of crabs, shrimp, and many other crustaceans feed on even smaller members of the plankton.

New generations of mole crabs

Mole crabs mate in spring and early summer. It is not unusual during that period to find two or three male crabs clinging to the smooth shell, or *carapace*, of the female. The males have special legs with suction disks for this purpose. Males are attracted only to females carrying unfertilized eggs. Hence, scientists believe that the eggs release into the waves a substance that attracts the males.

Females carry egg masses cemented on abdominal appendages. At first the eggs are orange. When they become grayish, they have turned into well-developed larvae. The females now stay quite low on the beach to protect the larvae from heat and to give them plenty of oxygen from the water. Finally the young set off into the ocean, strange

Waving tentacles crown the head of an inch-and-a-half-long sabellarian worm as it protrudes from its delicate sand-grain tube. Although individual tubes can easily be crushed between the fingertips, an active colony seldom shows any sign of damage or erosion from the constant pounding of the waves.

Vacant tubes such as those at the left become filled with sand and silt. Since the reef offers a solid support along a sandy beach, it is readily adopted by many smaller worms and crustaceans.

REEF-BUILDING WORMS THRIVE IN SURF

Instead of avoiding the pounding waves, sabellarian worms construct reefs squarely in their path. The tube-dwelling worms depend on waves to bring them both food and building materials. To start a reef, their planktonic larvae must first attach to some small but solid support—perhaps a stone or simply an outcropping of firm clay—in the lowest tidal region along a sandy beach. Using sand stirred up by the turbulent water, each worm constructs a tube by cementing the grains together with a mucuslike secretion. As worm after worm attaches to the support or to older tubes, the porous mass of closely packed tubes gradually enlarges until it may extend many yards across the beach. Secure in the protection of their tubes, the adult worms extend their heads into the waves and ensnare food particles with their tentacles.

Like a mass of porous sandstone, a sabellarian reef thrusts out from a stone breakwater in the headlong rush of waves. Active tubes are in the foreground, and old deserted tubes to the rear.

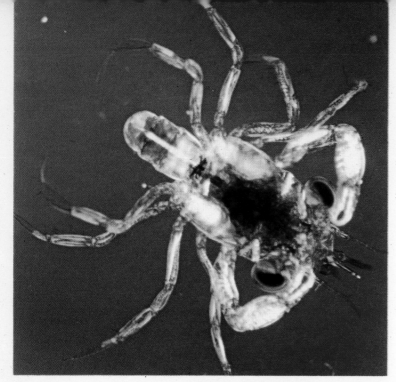

On completion of the zoea stage, mole crabs and other higher crustaceans transform into megalops larvae similar to the one shown here. After further growth, the megalops larva will settle to the bottom and transform into an adult.

little creatures that do not in the least resemble their parents. Each larva, known as a *zoea*, has a long tail and sharp spines and looks like the larvae of the vast majority of relatives of the mole crab—true crabs, shrimps, lobsters, and the like.

Where a zoea goes is anyone's guess. Too small and weak to swim against any water movement, it simply becomes one "mote" in the plankton. Like any of its drifting neighbors, it may be eaten by one of the kinds of marine animals that graze in these rich pastures of the sea. Mole crabs produce enough zoea, however, to keep shore populations high. Eventually the little larvae, which have been eating even smaller members of the plankton, come into shore having grown larger. This form, known as *megalops*, resembles the adult mole crab, except that in this stage its telson and abdomen are held out in a straight line. For a time it alternately swims and burrows in the sand, but after further growth it settles into the sand and seldom swims.

Mole crabs live at most a year and a few months, although nearly all of the males die before a year is up. At times the sea destroys huge populations of mole crabs. The most common danger is a severe storm that casts crabs by the thousands high up on the beach. Then sea birds and shore birds descend in great numbers. A day or two later all you will be able to find are countless mole crab shells rattling in the breeze among strands of dried seaweed in the beach wrack.

26

Even these skeletons are useful to one form of life. Most insects cannot stand the heat and salt at the beach, but some special forms, usually beetles, earwigs, and fly larvae, live along the top of the beach, never going far inland and never nearer the sea. If the shells of mole crabs are not too dry, beetles and other insect scavengers may be found nibbling on them.

The pulse of the world

Even more important than the effect of waves on the shore is the effect of tides. To see how they influence the many forms of shore life, start at low tide, which is by far the best time for study because many shore animals and plants are exposed.

If you can spend days or weeks at the shore, you may begin to discover patterns of behavior based on tides. Some animals, such as certain snails, limpets, and fiddler crabs, move about only when the tide is out. Others, such as oysters, mussels, and barnacles, close up when exposed to air and feed or change places only when covered by water. Sandpipers, mole crabs, swimming crabs, shore fishes, and others follow the tide level as it rises and falls.

The changing tides

When you visit different coastal areas you may notice that tides do not occur in the same patterns. The most familiar are regular, twice-daily tides, which reach their highest

Hundreds of gulls flock to a tidal flat in Washington state, attracted by the bountiful harvest of crustaceans and other animals exposed by the falling tide. Their banquet will continue until rising tide once again floods the area.

TIDES IN THE
BAY OF FUNDY

A salmon weir in the Bay of Fundy provides dramatic evidence of the effect of tides. Near the head of the Bay of Fundy, which lies between Nova Scotia and New Brunswick in Canada, the tidal range of fifty to sixty feet is the greatest in the world. The spectacular tides result largely from the shape of the bay. The immense volume of water flowing into the bay's broad mouth at high tide is forced to pile up on itself as it funnels into the narrower, shallower area toward the head of the bay.

Tides result from the gravitational pull of the moon and, to a lesser extent, the sun. These forces cause the waters of the oceans to form immense bulges on both sides of the earth. As the earth rotates beneath the bulges, the water level alternately rises and falls along coastlines, completing the cycle twice daily in most areas. (The contours of a coastline and its relation to the ocean basin beyond can modify the effect of the tide in a particular area.) When the sun and the moon lie in a direct line with the earth (twice a month), their combined gravitational attraction results in the exceptionally large tides known as spring tides. When they lie at right angles to the earth (also twice a month), the sun counteracts the attractive force of the moon and the effect is the relatively small tides known as neap tides.

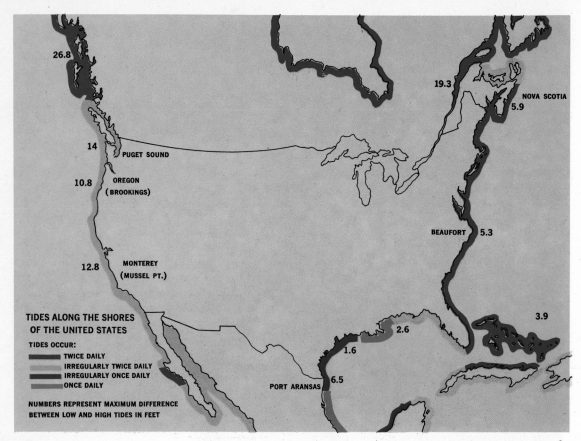

point every twelve hours and twenty-five minutes. Such tides take place on the open shores of the Atlantic coast from Nova Scotia to southern Florida. On most of the Pacific coast tides rise and fall twice a day, but not so regularly as along the Atlantic. The same thing happens on the west coast of Florida and the eastern half of the Gulf of Mexico. Around the Mississippi delta, however, tides occur regularly only once a day. Just to the west, along the Texas coast, tides also occur only once a day, but irregularly.

The long, narrow Bay of Fundy, on the east coast of Canada, has spectacular tides. The rise and fall may be over fifty feet, whereas at Key West, Florida, it is only one foot. In any river, upstream tides are likely to be delayed and have a greater rise and fall than those closer to the ocean. For example, the tidal rise and fall of nearly eight feet at Philadelphia occurs several hours later than the four-foot rise at the mouth of Delaware Bay. As this variety shows, the slope of the coast and the compressing effects of a narrow bay and river have almost as much effect as the moon and sun on the timetables and heights of tides.

A fish that comes ashore

One of the remarkable aspects of tidal rhythms is the fact that many sea and shoreline creatures have built into their systems "clocks" that follow changes in the tides. If you are in California in the spring or summer, particularly in the Cabrillo National Monument at San Diego, you can watch a striking event that shows this. At precisely high tide on the second, third, and fourth nights after the highest tides of each lunar month from April to August, the beaches swarm with thousands of small fish known as *grunion*. They swim in with the waves, wriggle up onto wet sand above the water line and begin to lay pods of eggs several inches beneath the surface of the sand. The males fertilize the eggs as the females deposit them, and the fish then return to the sea.

For two weeks the embryos grow within the eggs. Then they hatch—but only if they are washed by the high tides of the next dark moon. If this does not happen, they are able to wait another two weeks for the next high tide.

This astonishing spawning trait gives the grunion special advantages. Spawning occurs at night, when predatory birds are inactive. Buried in the sand, the developing eggs are protected from gulls and also from marine predators, which cannot get so far up the beach because the tides following the spawning nights are progressively lower. The eggs develop in a moist, fairly cool place, unaffected by waves. If spawning took place at the very highest tides of the lunar month, it would be at least a month, possibly two or more, until water would reach the eggs to wash the hatched fish out to sea. After the highest tide, waves carry sand in and deposit it, building up the beach. But just before the highest tides of the next cycle, waves carry sand off and erode the beach. It is this erosion that finally does wash out the small, newly hatched grunion, which are by this time capable of swimming away.

A living fossil

If you can more easily visit the beaches of the Middle Atlantic states rather than the West Coast, you can witness an even more impressive event than grunion spawning, one that has been going on for millions of years longer. In this

Precisely attuned to the rhythm of the tides, grunion spawn on California beaches only on certain nights during the spring and summer months. Wriggling tail-first into wet sand above the water line, the female deposits her eggs while the male, curled about her body, covers them with milt.

31

On nights of the highest tides in May and June, horseshoe crabs temporarily abandon the sea along the Atlantic coast, the smaller males clinging to the females. The female in the lower picture is about to excavate a nest in the sand.

case it is not a fish but the horseshoe "crab" that lays its eggs. This animal is really not a crab; it is a distant relative of the spiders. The only near relatives of this strange creature belong to two other species in the far Pacific. The horseshoe crab is a living fossil, a representative of a group of animals that has existed for over half a billion years—long before there were dinosaurs, and long, long before there were mammals or men. The Atlantic species, *Limulus polyphemus*, has not changed for approximately 150 million years!

Although *Limulus* lives in the Atlantic from Nova Scotia to Yucatán in Mexico, its densest population is in Delaware Bay. There four or five million animals were once harvested annually for fertilizer. Now the chemical-fertilizer industry has made gathering the horseshoe crab unprofitable, so it will probably continue to survive.

Limulus spends the winter in deeper water. In spring it begins to head for shore, not swimming but crawling over the ocean bottom, making good headway during flood tides. On nights of the new moon in May and June, and especially during the full moon, *Limulus* comes ashore on the high tide by the hundreds of thousands. The females, accompanied by the males, lumber up the beach, scoop out a shallow nest, and deposit several thousand eggs. Waves carry sperm from the males to fertilize the eggs. When the tide ebbs, the horseshoe crabs retreat with the water and seek the safety of the bay. Those that fail to make it force themselves into the sand to wait for the next high tide. But not all of them survive, for gulls may find them at daybreak and flip them over to eat the soft underside.

Predators also find the eggs developing in the moist sand. Crabs, fish, plovers, crows, and sandpipers often expose the

In a shallow nest in the sand, a female horseshoe crab deposits several thousand eggs, each about an eighth of an inch in diameter. Waves will bathe the eggs with sperm from the males and cover the nest with a protective layer of sand.

33

nests and consume thousands of the small greenish eggs. For those that survive, however, development is rapid in the warmth of the beach, and within a few days the membrane surrounding each egg splits and the egg inflates to several times its former size. If you find eggs in this condition, you will be able to look through the transparent covering and see in each a tiny horseshoe crab twisting about and feebly waving its legs. Within two weeks the young animals are ready to hatch. When a flooding tide lays bare the nest, churning sand grains cut open the egg membrane and set the larvae free. Within a short time the larvae molt their outer skin, develop a short tail, and move off across the bottom of the bay, where they find food and grow by molting periodically. Nine or ten years pass before they are mature enough to return to the beach to repeat the reproductive process.

If you have a chance to watch thousands of these cumbersome animals crawl laboriously up the beach on a spring night, you cannot escape the feeling that you are witnessing an event that reaches back ages before the dawn of any intelligence capable of watching and wondering. No other event on the shores of today's world so conveys the impression of great antiquity.

Living clocks

Egg-laying by the grunion and the horseshoe crab are two examples of the fascinating phenomenon known as *biological clocks*. Like many other biological-clock mechanisms (though by no means all), they are related to the tides. Biological clocks, or the rhythms of living things, probably exist in every cell of every plant and animal in the world. While we know little about most of them, there are many dramatic examples along the shoreline in addition to those of the grunion and *Limulus*. The reproductive activity of certain seaweeds and the feeding of oysters, clams, and

Fiddler crabs change color twice a day: their bodies are light at night, much darker by day. Only males possess enlarged foreclaws, which function in mating displays but are useless for feeding.

DARK PHASE

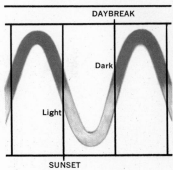

DAYBREAK

Dark

Light

SUNSET

LIGHT PHASE

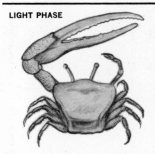

A few days after fertilization, the greenish outer membrane on the egg of a horseshoe crab splits open and the egg swells to the size of a small pea. Within the transparent inner membrane, the active embryo will continue to develop until, two weeks after the egg was laid, sand grains churning at high tide cut through this membrane and liberate the larva.

35

snails all show definite timing. Life cycles of most shoreline animals, in fact, can be considered clock mechanisms, though not all these "clocks" are set precisely.

If you should ever be near a salt marsh at low tide, stop and stay quietly in one spot for a time. You may see a flurry of activity as a dozen or more fiddler crabs move through the grass. They stop at their holes, sample the silt for food, and possibly work a little on the burrow.

Come back a few hours later, when the tide is high but not necessarily flooding the homes of the crabs. There will be very little activity. By returning periodically at high and low tides, you will learn that the fiddler crab is most active at low tide and ranges farther afield in search of food. During high tide, it is likely to remain within its burrow.

Simultaneously, this interesting creature demonstrates a clock not related to the tide. If you cannot approach the crabs, you can note their color in the daytime with a pair of binoculars. Then return at night and shine a light on them. The difference is striking—they are much darker in the daytime than at night.

Thus their behavior follows the "moon clock," or tides, whereas their color changes according to the "sun clock," or day and night. These two rhythms are quite separate, so at different times during a month you may find light active crabs, dark active crabs, light quiet crabs, or dark quiet crabs.

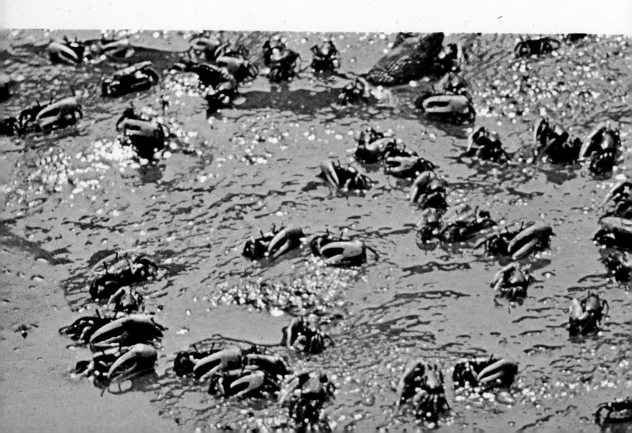

Worms and the moon

One of the most remarkable biological-clock mechanisms in the United States belongs to a worm, the Atlantic Palolo. This animal, *Eunice fucata*, has been studied on the coral shores of the Tortugas Islands off the southwestern tip of Florida, and also probably lives along the southern Florida Keys. Its strange name is taken from an even better-known worm of the South Pacific, the Palolo worm of Samoa, *Eunice viridis*.

The Atlantic Palolo lives in old coral reefs just below the low-tide mark. During its breeding period an astonishing thing happens. The rear part of the worm develops into a specialized reproductive portion that breaks off when mature and swims to the surface by itself. There hundreds of thousands of these "worms" release sperm and eggs. The eggs develop quickly into microscopic swimming larvae; these grow and then settle to the bottom in the porous limestone, where they create burrows and remain the rest of their lives.

Even more remarkable than the Atlantic Palolo's strange method of reproduction is the clock mechanism that sets it into action. The reproductive part of the worm comes to the surface at one very definite time during the year: before sunrise within three days of the moon's last quarter, between June 29 and July 28. In this brief time, shallow water near

Fiddler crabs swarm across the mud flats at low tide and retreat to their burrows when the tide rises. Even when they are placed in tubs with unchanging water levels, they continue to respond to the tidal rhythms of the flats where they were captured.

the shore comes alive with twisting, swarming worm fragments.

Tidal fluctuation in the area is minor. What, then, triggers the clock of the worms into action on precisely the same night of the lunar cycle each year? There are seasonal influences, of course, having to do with summer as opposed to other seasons. But the final "alarm" for the clock is the series of moonlight nights just before spawning time. Careful laboratory experiments with worms have shown that if the moonlight is artificially changed, the breeding time changes.

What are these biological clocks?

The swollen rear portion of this male Palolo worm's body is ready to break off and swim to the surface, where it will mingle with the reproductive portions of thousands of other worms.

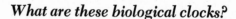

Although scientists have shown that occurrences in the environment not only start but also reset the clocks, no one really knows yet just how they run or why they do reset. Certainly the clocks are part of the inherited makeup of every living thing (some people can even "set" an alarm in their minds when they go to bed and wake up exactly at the time they want to). Through elaborate experiments, scientists have shown that both changes in form (*metamorphosis*) of an animal as it matures and clock mechanisms are controlled chemically inside the animal by substances known as *hormones*. These are manufactured by both plants and animals. It is possible to find shoreline animals, as well as those elsewhere, that respond on a schedule to light, temperature, experience, weak electrical fields, the earth's extremely weak magnetism, and even cosmic radiation, which comes from far out in space and can be detected by man only with delicate instruments. These subtle influences help work the biological clocks among the animals at the seashore, but probably the most important single factor in setting the clocks, after day and night, is the tide.

If shore creatures react to tides so markedly, why doesn't

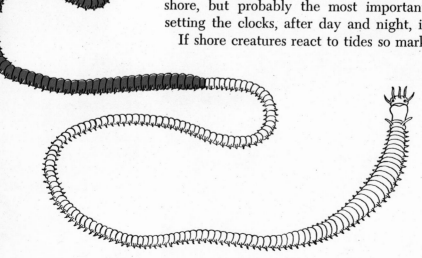

man feel the same influence? Theoretically we might, but the force of the earth's gravity is nine million times greater than the pull of the sun or moon on our bodies. Not being any longer in or dependent upon the water and its movements, we have lost our fishlike ancestors' ability to detect the tide or the forces that make it.

And though today we consider ourselves very clever, we have neglected to take advantage of the great power in the tide. The simpler animals of the shoreline have become adapted to it and depend upon it, but only now is man beginning to harness the tide. So far he has not been very successful in building power stations for this purpose, but a new, much larger effort of this sort is being made in France: an enormous dam is being built across the Rance Estuary through which it is hoped that the ebb and flow of the tides can be channeled to turn great turbines and provide power for people living in a nearby area hundreds of square miles in extent.

Native to warm southern waters, a Portuguese man-of-war cast ashore on a northern beach offers mute evidence of the existence of currents. These coelenterate animals cannot swim, but the Gulf Stream occasionally carries them all the way to Great Britain.

Rivers in the sea

Waves are one kind of water movement, the tides another. But there are still other ways in which water moves and thereby affects the life of the seashore.

You are beachcombing along the Atlantic coast and you have found a strange balloon, colored delicately pink and blue. Don't touch it! It is the float and sail of the Portuguese man-of-war, an unusual grouping of polyps, some of which possess extremely dangerous stings. It is no jellyfish (which can also sting), as some beach visitors think. The Portuguese man-of-war is usually found in warm tropical or semitropical waters. What is it doing on a beach in Virginia or Cape Cod?

Look out to sea and you may find a few more floating in the water. Suppose the day is windless and the waves low. Although these colonies cannot swim, they still parade slowly past, parallel to the shore. They are being carried not by waves and not by tides, but by currents. Currents, aided perhaps by the wind, are the only explanation for their presence so far north.

While watching crowds of mole crabs on the beach, you may have noticed that there are many in some places, none in others. Perhaps you noted one large group, but on returning a day or two later you found it gone. Although mole

crabs appear to move only up and down the beach with waves and tides, currents flowing along the shoreline carry them the length of the beach as well.

To see how the *longshore currents* affect life, examine a sample of water carefully. You may find pieces of marsh plants miles from the nearest inlet. This is proof that currents—as well as tides—distribute vital nutrients from the land throughout the coastal area. The mole crab and other animals that strain water live on plankton and other food carried great distances from their original sources.

Another bit of scientific reasoning will add to your knowledge of currents: for hundreds of miles along a coast the same populations of fixed plants and animals appear wherever conditions will support them. How did they get there? Few can ever swim against moving water. All, however, pass through larval or spore stages that drift with the longshore currents. Millions upon millions of eggs, larvae, and plant spores travel this way. You may happen upon a clam shedding its eggs or a rockweed its spores. The mass of eggs or the spores will drift out to sea, even at slack tide and even when the waves are quiet. Currents are still at work.

The mightiest of all currents are those that flow in more or less circular patterns around the oceans. Set in motion by the rotation of the earth, such ocean currents are the largest rivers in the world. The Gulf Stream and the Japan Current are the two that affect North American coasts. Our northeastern and northwestern states are warmed by these great currents, which bring heat from the tropics. Warm-water shore animals can live farther north than you might expect if the coasts are bathed by currents from the south. At the point where the great currents finally leave the shore and veer out to sea, the populations of shoreline animals change markedly.

An unusual colony of specialized individuals, the Portuguese man-of-war trails its lethal stinging tentacles as much as forty feet below the gas-filled float. When a fish becomes entangled in the tentacles, it is instantly paralyzed by venom from the stinging cells. The tentacles then retract and carry the fish up to the mouths of the feeding individuals.

NORTH PACIFIC CURRENT

LABRADOR CURRENT

NORTH ATLANTIC DRIFT

GULF STREAM

CALIFORNIA CURRENT

CANARIES CURRENT

NORTH EQUATORIAL CURRENT

NORTH EQUATORIAL CURRENT

EQUATORIAL COUNTERCURRENT

SOUTH EQUATORIAL CURRENT

SOUTH EQUATORIAL CURRENT

HUMBOLDT CURRENT

BRAZIL CURRENT

WEST WIND DRIFT

WARM CURRENTS

Driven by prevailing winds, the great global currents flow in sweeping circular patterns around the oceans of the world, clockwise in the Northern Hemisphere, counterclockwise south of the equator. Blowing diagonally toward the equator in both hemispheres, trade winds move the equatorial currents steadily to the west across both the Atlantic and Pacific until finally the water is deflected by land barriers. Farther from the equator, the westerlies blow steadily toward the east in both hemispheres. Although winds are the primary driving force, several other factors contribute to current

OCEAN CURRENTS OF THE WORLD

NORTH PACIFIC CURRENT

JAPAN CURRENT

INDIAN COUNTERCURRENT

SOUTH EQUATORIAL CURRENT

WEST AUSTRALIAN CURRENT

EAST AUSTRALIAN CURRENT

...D CURRENTS ➡ PREVAILING WINDS ➡

patterns. As the sun heats the ocean surface in the tropics, the water becomes lighter and tends to flow toward the poles. (Cold, heavy water from the poles in turn flows toward the equator in sub-surface currents.) In addition, the earth's rotation on its axis exerts a deflecting influence on winds, currents, and on all moving things, causing them to veer to the right in the Northern Hemisphere and to the left south of the equator. Land masses also influence both over-all patterns and local de-flections of the currents that travel in great swirl-ing eddies around the oceans.

Currents from the deep

Along California cliffs, high above rocks and coves at the water's edge, you may see clouds of sea birds wheeling and diving over the deep water offshore. What attracts them?

If you go out in a boat beneath the birds, you can see multitudes of small fish swimming and feeding close to the surface. To see what they are feeding on, draw a small, fine-mesh net through the water. It will capture part of a rich plankton bloom of minute plants, small grazing worms, and tiny crustaceans. The plants of the plankton, like all other plants, grow and reproduce best where there is a rich supply of the minerals they need. These nutrients, mostly such chemicals as phosphates and nitrates, accumulate on the sea bottom from the rain of dead plants and animals that descends from the surface water. There the fertilizer lies, until, along the West Coast of the United States and off Peru in South America, like huge elevators great upwelling currents carry tons of nutrients to the surface. Deep currents have to rise as the bottom grows shallower near the land, so concentrations of nutrients rise just offshore and the local plankton blooms abundantly. Small fish gather to eat the plankton, and birds arrive to feed on the fish.

Where upwelling currents are particularly strong, small weird fish of the abyss (the great ocean depths) are occasionally found at the surface.

A mixing of waters

Some coastal currents start with a river. From a high vantage point near the mouth of a bay, you may see streaks of colored water where a river flows into the sea. The junction of river and sea creates a dangerous, turbulent current known as a *rip*, which is particularly evident when the tide moves in or out. And there are still other effects where a river empties into the ocean.

First, a river carries suspended sediment from land into the sea. Out beyond the mouth of a bay, the water clears. The current of a river is slowed when it meets the water of the sea and can no longer carry all the silt. Particles drop down, slowly and gently blanketing wide regions of the bay and also the relatively shallow region beyond, the con-

A flock of pelicans traces a line of white above Pacific waters on the California coast. Many birds congregate here to feed on fish that thrive where nutrient-rich upwelling currents support abundant plankton populations.

45

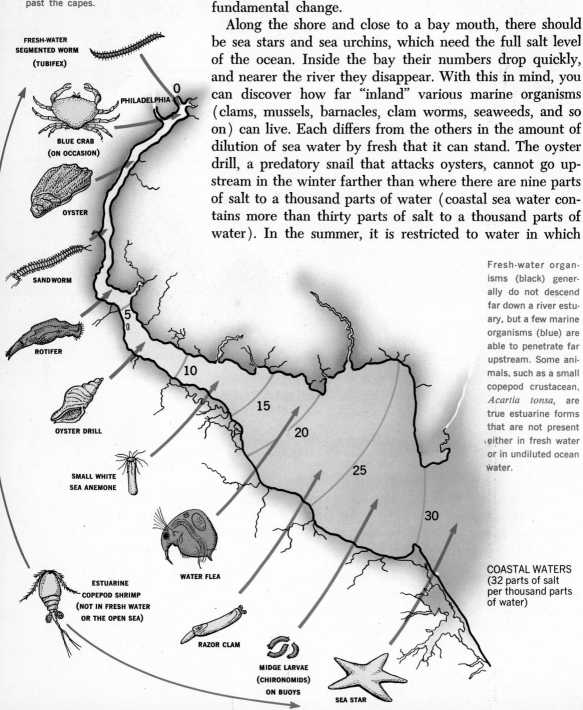

An estuary is a river in which fresh water flowing from the land mixes with ocean water surging in with the tides, producing graded dilutions of salt water. The approximate salinities for the Delaware River estuary are shown here as parts of salt per thousand parts of water. The result is a salinity gradient that stretches ninety miles from Philadelphia (at the top of the map) out past the capes.

tinental shelf. The bottom of a bay, of course, is not clean-washed sand, but a mixture of sand, silt, clay, mud, and the remains of plants and animals. The animals that live here differ from those that must have the clean bottoms and clear water of the open shore of the ocean.

Then the river's fresh water gradually combines with the salt water of the sea. It is interesting to try to trace the slow change from fresh to salt water. The plants and animals of the shore and the bay flats provide clues to this fundamental change.

Along the shore and close to a bay mouth, there should be sea stars and sea urchins, which need the full salt level of the ocean. Inside the bay their numbers drop quickly, and nearer the river they disappear. With this in mind, you can discover how far "inland" various marine organisms (clams, mussels, barnacles, clam worms, seaweeds, and so on) can live. Each differs from the others in the amount of dilution of sea water by fresh that it can stand. The oyster drill, a predatory snail that attacks oysters, cannot go upstream in the winter farther than where there are nine parts of salt to a thousand parts of water (coastal sea water contains more than thirty parts of salt to a thousand parts of water). In the summer, it is restricted to water in which

Fresh-water organisms (black) generally do not descend far down a river estuary, but a few marine organisms (blue) are able to penetrate far upstream. Some animals, such as a small copepod crustacean, *Acartia tonsa*, are true estuarine forms that are not present either in fresh water or in undiluted ocean water.

FRESH-WATER SEGMENTED WORM (TUBIFEX)

PHILADELPHIA

0

BLUE CRAB (ON OCCASION)

OYSTER

SANDWORM

5

0

ROTIFER

10

OYSTER DRILL

15

20

SMALL WHITE SEA ANEMONE

25

30

WATER FLEA

ESTUARINE COPEPOD SHRIMP (NOT IN FRESH WATER OR THE OPEN SEA)

RAZOR CLAM

COASTAL WATERS
(32 parts of salt per thousand parts of water)

MIDGE LARVAE (CHIRONOMIDS) ON BUOYS

SEA STAR

the salt is not less than fifteen parts per thousand. The oyster can stand much lower dilutions and so lives upstream of the "drill line," quite free from this predator.

Most of the salt in sea water is sodium chloride, common table salt, but there are other salts and minerals. Nearly fifty elements have been identified in ocean water. If you allow a dish of sea water to evaporate, you can see crystals of this residue. Evaporate a similar amount of bay water and less dry salt results. Water from the mouth of the river would have very little salt. By allowing equal amounts of water from different distances seaward from the river to evaporate, you can get some idea of how the salt increases toward the sea. Tasting the water, if it isn't too dirty, is also a rough but useful test, particularly if you have several containers of water from different places side by side. Scientists, of course, have accurate and reliable means of determining the exact salt content of sea water.

After a heavy rain, silt-laden waters of the Russian River in northern California stain the surface of the Pacific Ocean. As the silt particles settle from the water, they will add to the accumulation of sediment on the ocean bottom at the mouth of the river.

47

The shore at night

So far, we have been visiting the seashore in the bright light of the summer sun. Yet there is another, equally fascinating shore world that is less familiar to most people. When night falls the life of a beach undergoes a remarkable change.

Where are the birds that were so plentiful during the day? Terns, skimmers, sandpipers, plovers, willets, and other shore birds sleep quietly in marshes or on the dunes. Gulls float in protected bay waters or sleep at the water's edge. Back in the dunes in the early evening you may hear whippoorwills and, later at night, possibly the hooting of an owl. These are the only birds now active.

In fact, except for occasional owls, there are no birds flying over the shoreline. But skunks, rats, minks, and raccoons come to the water's edge, especially during low tide, to forage among the exposed mussels, oysters, worms, and whatever fish or crustaceans have been trapped in pools left by the outgoing tide. Finding these mammals is hard, even with powerful lights, for they are wary and leave when man is near. Usually only their tracks will tell you of their presence.

The best time to go out at night is at low tide. You need a good light—the best kind fastens around your head by a band and the batteries hang on your belt. The connecting wire should pass beneath your sweater or jacket so it won't interfere with your arms. Shoes are important. Wear rough-soled sneakers that can get wet, for at night most reflections disappear and a tidal pool can look like dry land—you will step in one more than once. Old, warm clothes are necessary,

Tracks of the dune-dwelling beach mouse trace a delicate pattern across the sand. The mouse itself is seldom seen since it spends the day hidden in its burrow.

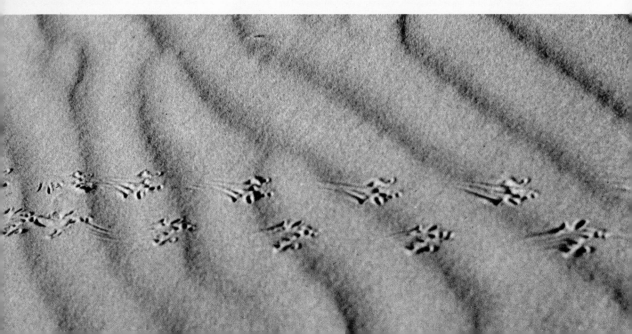

for most shores cool off at night, even in midsummer. A plastic bucket makes a good collecting container and is far safer than glass bottles, which may break in your pockets if you fall. The best net is a small aquarium type that can lift animals from tide pools without great disturbance.

An underwater flashlight can be a rewarding tool. If you wade in shallow water, the light will reveal animal activity not visible from the surface.

High on the beach, ghost crabs scurry about in search of food, particularly in the beach wrack. You can come quite close to one by shining the light directly on it while walking

At night raccoons and many other land animals emerge from hiding and walk along the water's edge, searching for mussels, crabs, shrimp, and other food.

The moon rising above the coast of Olympic National Park, Washington.

From its tunnel in the dry sand above high tide, a dune wolf spider ventures out at night to prey on insects that forage in the beach wrack. A silken webbing anchors the sand in place at the entrance to its burrow.

slowly toward it. Keep the light ahead, without passing your hand in front of it, and the crab will "freeze" until it can see some kind of movement. You should be able to get within a foot or so, near enough to study its form.

Animals of the night

In addition to crabs and small mammals on land, swimming types that dwell in shallow water come in much closer to shore and often can be watched with ease from close to the edge of the water. Shrimps and smaller crustaceans can be seen swimming or crawling over the bottom more easily at night.

Fish of many kinds feed in the shallowest water at low tide—killifish, sculpins, anchovies, silversides, needlefish, dogfish, skates, and a host of others. In Florida or southern California waters, a flashlight may reveal sea hares swimming slowly by, flapping large "wings." These creatures are actually giant snails that have no external shells. A small school of squid may dart into view and out again just as suddenly.

On shore at night, along the rocks, snails and limpets leave their niches to browse on algae, traveling farther than they do at low tide in the daytime. In the realm of the ghost crab, high on a sandy beach, beach hoppers (or sand fleas) are energetically seeking food in the decaying matter cast up earlier by the high tide. Many of the insects of the upper beach will be active in the same general area. Large dune wolf spiders range down from their high ground in dry sand to capture these insects.

Even though it may be hard to see in the water, you can demonstrate that small crustaceans change their day and night locations. For example, certain small shrimps that you can catch quite easily in a fine net, the *mysids*, spend their days close to the bottom, where they feed along the sand and in decaying material. At night, however, they become members of the plankton and can be caught with a net near

After a night of feeding on dead material cast ashore by the tide, a quarter-inch-long beach hopper excavates a burrow in the sand on the upper beach. On the following night the tiny amphipod will abandon this shelter, feed again, and then dig a new burrow.

the surface. This is true of a number of other small crus-taceans, especially copepods, isopods, and amphipods. In fact, of a selected group of planktonic animals, 93 per cent are most abundant close to the surface at night, and only 7 per cent are most abundant in the daytime.

The situation with plant plankton seems to be just the reverse. If you use a plankton net and examine your catch through a microscope, you will find that the one-cell plants known as *diatoms* are much less abundant close to the surface at night than in the daytime. The reason is obvious. These yellowish-brown microscopic organisms, being plants, are photosynthetic and need light with which to manu-facture their fuel and food. How they, as nonswimmers, migrate up and down in the water is still being studied by biologists.

Going along the shore night after night, you will begin to recognize patterns in the different activities of animals. Some animals you will come to recognize as *nocturnal* (nighttime) and others as *diurnal* (daytime). As you come to know them better, you will realize that animals even act differently on moonlight nights than they do on nights with-out a visible moon.

Spring

The most fortunate seashore observers are those who live at the shore all year round. They can watch the slow turn of the seasons with all the beauty and mystery it brings. On the shore no less than in the garden or in the forest, the changes are dramatic.

In spring, perhaps the most obvious sign of the warm weather to come is the reappearance of certain shore birds. Gulls leave inland lakes and ponds where many of them spend the winter, and take up life along the shores and in-lets once more. Along some protected bay shores there may be greater concentrations of gulls in winter than in sum-mer. The long-legged shore birds and terns begin to arrive

— ANIMAL PLANKTON

— PLANT PLANKTON

In shallow coastal waters that are not violently agitated by currents or waves, animal plankton remains near the bottom during the day and then migrates to the surface at night. Plant plankton, on the other hand, remains near the surface during the day and tends to sink somewhat at night, but usually not to the bottom.

Like many other small crustaceans, a half-inch-long mysid shrimp migrates from the bottom to the surface of the water at night—in some cases a journey of as much as twenty or thirty feet.

55

from the South; some come from great distances, others may fly only a few hundred miles north.

Fishing records show that along the Atlantic coast an exchange takes place between pairs of species of certain types of fish. Winter flounders and winter skates leave the bays and summer flounders and skates take their places.

Horseshoe crabs come into bays along the Atlantic, and on both coasts certain swimming crabs penetrate the shallower waters as they warm up. Shore-breeding fish, such as the Atlantic menhaden, appear in huge numbers from no one knows where in the ocean, churning the water and turning it pink with schools of millions. Along the shoreline, particularly on rocks and pilings, new hydroid colonies begin to grow, and attached seaweeds grow longer and thicker.

Wild flowers spangle the dunes with gold as spring arrives on the Oregon coast. Less obvious, but more important, is the explosive springtime increase in plant plankton in the offshore water, since the plankton will provide food for the larvae of a multitude of shore and shallow-water animals.

The nest of a tern may be a well-built mass of vegetation or, as in this case, simply a shallow depression in the sand. Within hours of hatching, the chick's wet down becomes dry and fluffy.

The floating plants and the plankton quite suddenly bloom in enormous quantities. Why? Nutrients that have lain on the bottom during the colder months now are carried to the surface by rising currents created by the warming weather.

Using a simple plankton net you can trace the change. First you notice the blooms of plant plankton. Then, after a while, you will begin to catch increasing numbers of animal plankton, which graze upon this crop of the sea. For a while the bulk of the animal plankton consists of larval forms of almost every kind of shoreline and shallow-water animal—mole crabs, horseshoe crabs, true crabs, shrimps, worms of all types, clams, snails, sea stars, sea urchins, hydroids, and many others. This is the season of the sea's babies, and never again during the year will the zooplankton (animal plankton) contain so many different animal forms. Even if you can visit the shore in spring for only a day, it is worth taking a plankton sample to examine under your magnifying lenses.

Summer

Then comes summer. The shoreline algae grow large and cover rocks and jetties. Attached hydroids, mussels, and other animals compete for space. Eventually the overcrowding becomes so severe that many individuals die.

57

Gannets space their nests with almost geometric precision in this breeding colony on an island in the Gulf of St. Lawrence. After the nesting season, the birds are seen occasionally along the Atlantic coast, soaring on wings with a six-foot span. They capture fish by plunging directly into the water.

Along the shores birds are constantly busy. Although some nested in spring, most will be found nesting in early summer, high on the beaches and in the dunes. Others perch on rocky cliffs, where they lay conical eggs on narrow shelves. If you take a plankton tow just offshore, you discover that the plant plankton has diminished, mostly because the nutrients are used up temporarily. Animal plankton continues to increase, however, partly due to the many larvae, but also because some of the larvae turn into planktonic adults. In the early summer you will find many zooplankton forms changing (metamorphosing) from one state into another. You can, for example, trace the development of a crab from an elongated, spiny zoea through a series of stages to a broad, short crab.

Without question, summer is the season of peak animal activity along beaches and rocks, and in shallow water. Summer vacations at the shore can be more than a pleasant time in which to relax—they can be exciting as an introduction to a totally new and strange world.

Fall

Then fall comes, slowly ending the great activity of the summer. Swimming crabs leave the shore to migrate into deeper water where the temperature is more constant. Along rocks and pilings, the enormous numbers of hydroids now commence to do something besides feed. If you look closely at a hydroid colony under a magnifying lens, you will see many small capsules developing. Inside each capsule several tiny jellyfish, or *medusae*, are growing. When set free, they swim off as members of the plankton. Shoreline hydroid populations begin to die and disappear.

Summer skate and summer flounder leave, to be replaced by their winter counterparts. The number of migratory

SPRING

SUMMER

FALL

WINTER

After a sparse plankton population in the winter, spring plankton bursts forth with enormous numbers of diatoms and other plants. Although these diminish in the summer, they have provided food for the great numbers of animal plankton, both adults and larvae, that increase during warmer months. After another diatom bloom in the fall, plankton of both kinds reaches its lowest ebb in winter.

shore birds drops each day, although for a while those from more northerly regions stop by to take their places. Some of these northern birds may not continue on, but remain along milder shores for the winter.

Intertidal seaweeds diminish somewhat, although many forms persist quite unchanged through the winter. In early fall, however, other algae of the plankton go through another explosive bloom because dissolved nutrients built up during the summer once more collect near the surface. Animal plankton diminishes as fall wears on, and finally so does the plant plankton.

In fall the waters around the mouths of rivers grow saltier. Why? As less fresh water flows out of rivers in the drier season, the salt fronts of bays move farther upstream and affect the animals living there. Ocean species now invade bays and even penetrate river mouths. It may be difficult, however, to find out which changes in animal populations are due to altered salinity and which are due to the cooler temperatures.

Winter

Finally winter arrives, but this does not mean the shore should be avoided completely. You may have to dress warmly to withstand the biting winds, but the shore in winter in most areas of the United States is a fine place to observe birds. There are more laughing gulls and herring gulls. Often you will see birds that normally are not there during the warmer months. Scoters, brant, great black-backed gulls, ruddy turnstones, purple sandpipers, dunlins, and greater yellowlegs are just a few of the northern, even arctic, birds that spend their winters along the Atlantic coast. In the Gulf of Mexico, curlews and godwits from farther north feed in winter on the plentiful supplies of food thrown up by the waves.

Now it is hard to find smaller shore animals. They are either dormant and inactive or have vanished and are existing elsewhere in some other stage of their life cycles, perhaps as eggs or larval forms. Even the shallow-water plankton populations are at their lowest ebb.

Etched by the ebbing and flowing tide, the snow along the edge of a Massachusetts beach (as seen from the air) forms a gigantic saw-tooth pattern.

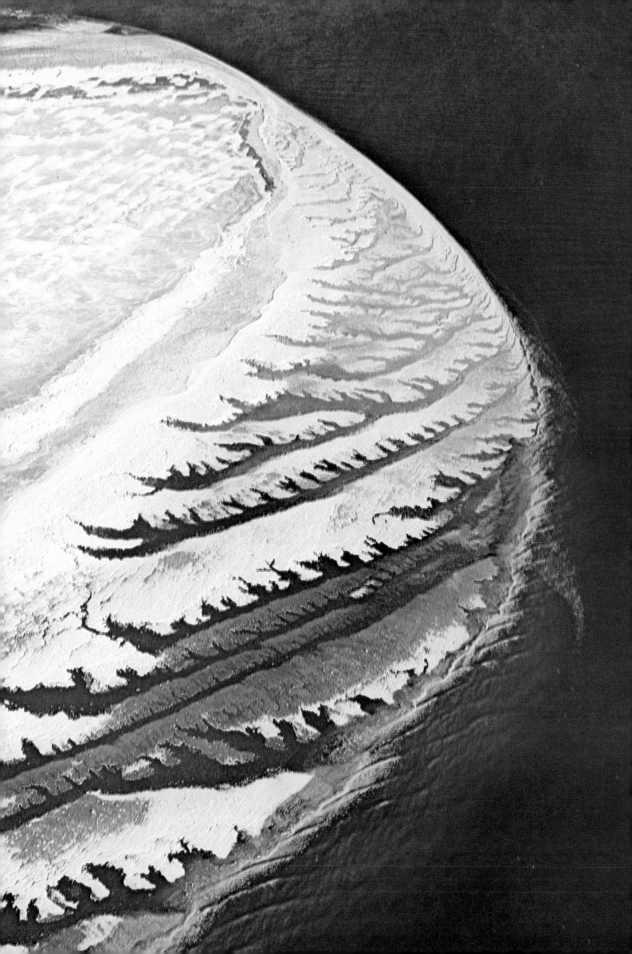

The shore in winter can be a place of desolate beauty, and you can depend upon finding vast stretches of beach without another human figure in sight. Sparse as some of the animal populations may be, this is one of the most rewarding times to walk along the shoreline. Even far south, along the lower California coast, the Florida Keys, and the Gulf coast, marked changes are apparent in the presence and activities of animals. If you keep a log of what you find, after a year of entries you should have a rewarding and predictable series of population changes—animal, plant, and even human.

Even in deepest winter a few gulls are evident in this icy seascape on Long Island Sound. In many areas the violent winter surf erodes the sand deposited on beaches by the gentler waves of summer.

The seashore—a world in motion

You have now seen that more than anything else, life at the shore must contend with water always in motion, often

moving with great force. To do so, shore plants and animals have an almost unlimited variety of specialized adaptations.

This is not all a matter of defense. Moving water is essential to shore life, for it brings food and oxygen, and carries away eggs, larvae, spores, and wastes. It is the sole means of transport for those small, weak, or nonswimming members of the plankton. Water is the basis for the wide spread of shore species on both coasts and around the world.

Two forces that give energy to the water are the whirling globe and the winds of the atmosphere, the latter set in motion by the sun's heat. A third major force is the gravitational pull of both sun and moon.

The slow, majestic course of the earth around the sun during a year, the more hurried monthly revolution of the moon about the earth, and the rapid turning of the earth on its own axis have their effects upon the life of the shore, making it the most fluctuating environment on our planet.

The Many
Worlds of
the Seashore

A seashore consists of many worlds—marsh mud, sand dunes, or rocky cliffs—all changing from age to age as well as from hour to hour.

Now let us return to a rocky cliff and to a sandy beach. We will also observe the hot desert sands of a traveling dune and the rich, highly populated world of a salt marsh and a tidal flat. Another shoreline environment we shall look at includes the miniature marine world of a tide pool, with its extreme condition of saltiness and heat. And we must not forget to consider the microscopic world of animals that live actively between the grains of sand.

The plants and animals in each of these habitats occupy zones of their own. With a little care in observation, you can quickly become skilled at recognizing not only a particular habitat but also the *zonation* of life within it. You can then predict what living things you are likely to find in specific localities.

Another phenomenon of the shore—one that also occurs in a pond, in a forest, and in all other natural environments —is *succession*. This is the process in which certain plants and animals first colonize a territory, and then are followed by different species until finally a stable, so-called climax community becomes established.

You can observe both by simply watching the scene as you drive to the shore.

Life on the sand dunes

If you are lucky as you approach a shoreline, you may come across a traveling dune a mile or more from the sea. How did it come to be so far from the water? Sometimes, wind, geography, climate, and other aspects of nature have combined to release the sand from the beach and move it inland. Sometimes man has burned off the original covering vegetation, leaving loose sand for the wind to blow inland. Eventually this sand turns into a miniature, rapidly traveling desert, covering roads, homesteads, ponds, fields, and even towns. For example, until recent years, the great traveling sand dune at Cape Henlopen on the Atlantic coast flowed west as much as sixty feet a year.

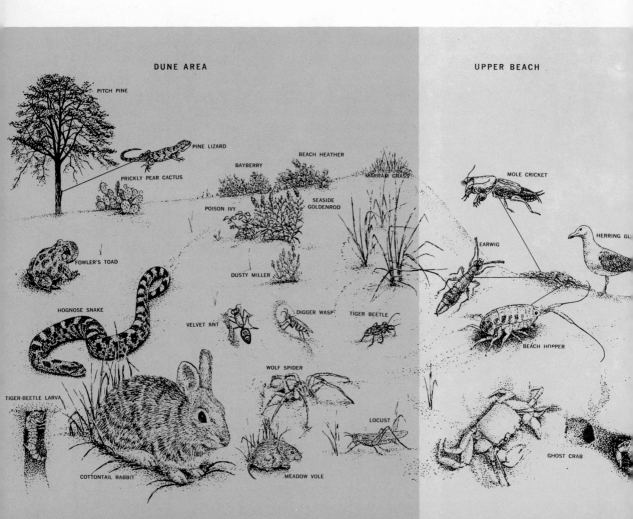

So far as its life is concerned, a traveling dune is a true desert. Find a spot without plants and look for animal life. At the height of the day you may see nothing; but animals, mostly mammals and insects, do appear when it is cooler—in the early morning, late afternoon, and evening.

Measure the air temperature over your head with a thermometer shaded by a piece of cardboard or wood. Measure it again at knee level and then at every couple of inches down to the sand. No wonder it seems hot on the dunes—as you get close to the sand the temperature shoots up. On a summer day it may pass 120° Fahrenheit. If the thermometer is long and narrow, push it into the sand and take a series of readings beneath the surface. The temperature should drop quickly. Sand a foot or so below the surface will be relatively cool.

But where will you find life? Look first in the air. You may see predatory robber flies, biting horseflies, and digger wasps flying across the dunes. Only the robber flies and wasps normally descend to the hot sand, where they grab other insects. Even robber flies usually capture prey on the

The zonation of life on a beach is distinct, but it often goes unseen. While the location of land plants is obvious, most of the animals shown here spend much of their time beneath the sand. Sea gulls, sandpipers, tiger beetles, digger wasps, velvet ants, and maritime locusts are examples of beach animals that may be active at noontime. Pine lizards, cottontail rabbits, and voles are active at dawn and dusk. Toads, hognose snakes, wolf spiders, ghost crabs, and beach hoppers are active through the night. Similar patterns of day–night activity are not so apparent beneath the water—habits and migrations of marine beach animals are governed largely by tides and by wave action. Clams left behind by an ebbing tide simply cease their feeding activity, but crabs and fish follow the water line and remain active twenty-four hours a day.

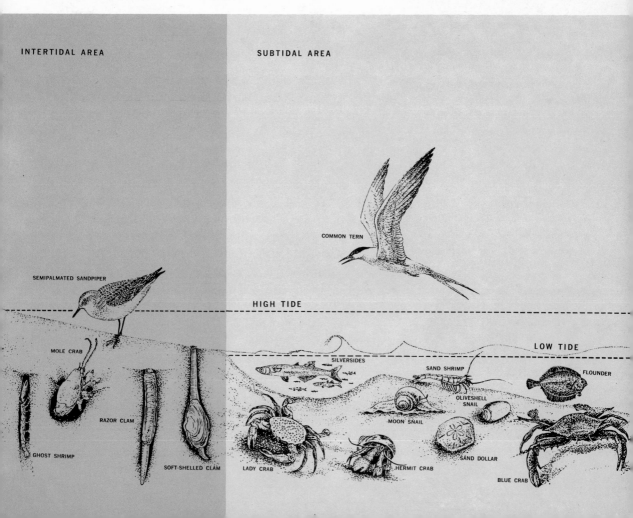

INTERTIDAL AREA

SUBTIDAL AREA

COMMON TERN

SEMIPALMATED SANDPIPER

HIGH TIDE

LOW TIDE

MOLE CRAB

SILVERSIDES

SAND SHRIMP

FLOUNDER

OLIVESHELL SNAIL

MOON SNAIL

RAZOR CLAM

GHOST SHRIMP

SOFT-SHELLED CLAM

LADY CRAB

HERMIT CRAB

SAND DOLLAR

BLUE CRAB

Enormous compound eyes almost cover the head of a horsefly. This inhabitant of the dunes can inflict a painful bite in its quest for blood.

A swift and agile climber, the pine lizard prefers the pitch-pine area to the hot sand of open dunes. Insects are the staple in its diet.

wing. The other flying insects perch on the sparse dune vegetation. Some of the wasps, however, escape the extreme surface heat by digging burrows in the sand.

Temperatures of 120 degrees can kill an insect by coagulating its body fluids, so these wasps must protect themselves when digging. Watch a small, blue-eyed, yellow-and-black-banded wasp known as *Bembex*. It digs furiously for a moment, like a dog throwing dirt back with its front legs. Then it rises into the air a few feet above the spot to cool off. It descends, digs, rises, and continues to do this until the burrow has entered cooler layers of sand. Later the wasp searches out dead insects, which it places in the burrow beside its eggs. When the larvae hatch, their food is waiting.

Your eye may be caught by a strange insect running across the blistering sand. It looks like a large, wingless, furry ant, and is even called a velvet ant. Actually, it is a wasp with a powerful sting. Several species that live on coastal dunes are brilliantly colored, but they are not playthings! Velvet ants lay their eggs in burrows of digger wasps.

The eggs hatch quickly and the young velvet ants then prey upon the digger-wasp larvae.

How does the velvet ant survive the heat? Its dense "fur" provides insulation by creating an airspace around its body. On an eastern dune the fur is scarlet and black; in the Southwest desert it may be white. A great many other dune and desert insects, including robber flies, tiger beetles, and wasps, have similar protection.

Where there is vegetation on a dune you will find a few creatures that feed on plants. These include the maritime locust (a grasshopper), rabbits, and mice. Predators are here much more common and include ant lions, which dig conical pits of loose sand that trap other insects, and swift tiger beetles; small, swift lizards; hawks and smaller birds; and foxes.

Leave an inland dune and walk toward the shore. Note how the vegetation changes. The increasing salt in the air drastically reduces the kinds of plants, for not many can stand it. Soon you arrive at the barrier dune, which rises high above the beach and prevents water from flooding flat regions inland. When storms destroy a barrier dune near populated areas, engineers and construction crews quickly rebuild it. Then the dune is replanted with marram grass or other kinds of vegetation that hold the sand in place.

When it captures an insect in the air over the dunes, a robber fly clasps the victim with its long legs and sucks out the body juices.

After digging a burrow in the sand, the half-inch-long digger wasp, or *Bembex*, deposits its eggs and provisions the burrow with dead insects.

A barrier dune, like a traveling dune, is caused by the prevailing wind, which lifts beach sand, especially the finest particles, and carries it inland. You can see this effect also in a wind "shadow" behind a rock or a bit of driftwood. Here, in the lee of the wind (the side opposite the direction the wind comes from), sand piles up in a long, miniature dune.

Writing in the sand

Now you have reached the beach itself. Here a fascinating story is written across the surface of the sand. The trick is to read it.

Back from the shore, on the barrier dune, you may find curious circular marks around tufts of marram grass. What are they? Wait for a breeze and watch a broken blade of grass twirl around, etching a perfect circle in the sand. Smooth sand above the high-tide mark often displays a variety of irregular, looping, spattering tracks. Though you may never discover the exact cause of each mark, you can see what has happened by setting free a bit of dried sponge, crumpled paper, or anything light in weight. It will leave tracks as the wind bounces it along.

Twirling blades of marram grass etch a circle in the sand— evidence of the wind that ceaselessly alters the world of the sand dunes.

You will, however, come across regular tracks that course about the sand in definite directions—animals make these. Tiny paths resembling a zipper are left by scavenger beetles living near the high-tide mark. Small dents in the sand surface near the beach wrack may be the impressions made by beach hoppers, or sand fleas.

If you come across a larger straight path made by many sharp toes, follow it. The tracks should end in a round, deep hole in the sand above the intertidal region. Sometimes the tracks radiate from the hole in all directions. Sit quietly nearby, or return at night, and you may see a ghost crab emerge from the hole, perhaps carrying a load of sand as it enlarges its burrow. At night the crabs travel far from home, scavenging along the beach and in the wrack for bits of food.

With legs that span almost ten inches, a frightened ghost crab can scuttle across the sand with amazing speed. When it stands still, its color blends so well with the sand that it seems to disappear before your eyes—hence its name.

Closely spaced ripple marks
such as these result from
currents; they usually lie
at right angles to the direction
of the current. Much wider
ripple marks, parallel to the
water's edge, are formed by the
backwash of waves in the
receding tide.

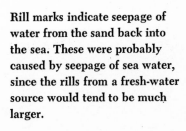

Rill marks indicate seepage of
water from the sand back into
the sea. These were probably
caused by seepage of sea water,
since the rills from a fresh-water
source would tend to be much
larger.

In the intertidal region, ripples and rills usually cover the
sand at low tide. The backwash of waves in the receding
tide leaves some ripples about eighteen inches apart and
parallel to the water's edge. Other ripples, one to three
inches apart, result from a longshore current; these usually
lie at right angles to the direction of the current.

There are small branching rills in the sand that are
minute rivers flowing to the sea. Put your finger in the
water and taste it. If it is salty, the water that has sunk
into the sand above during high tide is now draining out;
if it is fresh, water is seeping from farther inland.

The most familiar marks or tracks on the beach will be
those of birds foraging in the wet sand of the lower intertidal
region. There you will find the broad, triangular webbed
marks left by gulls and the delicate three-pronged toemarks
made by sandpipers, sanderlings, and other small birds. You
may even find signs of invaders from land. You can recognize
grackle and starling prints by the long hind toe, which the
bird scuffs over the sand. By following bird tracks you can
learn what the birds eat—perhaps you will find the remains
of a dead fish or a deep narrow hole where a sandpiper discovered a mole crab or a sandworm. In this way you can
figure out both the kind and number of some hidden populations.

73

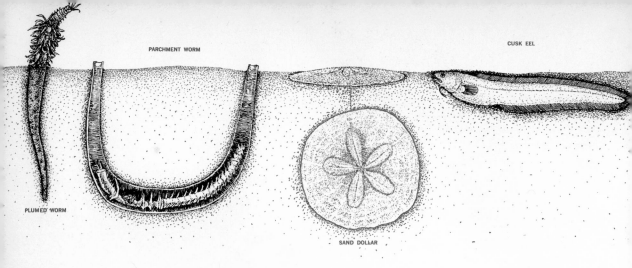

PARCHMENT WORM

CUSK EEL

PLUMED WORM

SAND DOLLAR

How to find life in the sand

But tracks and trails in the sand help you find only some of the hidden creatures. Many animals do not leave their burrows to crawl about, so you must be able to "read" the different kinds of holes, tubes, and burrows in the intertidal region. Some holes are made by water percolating down through the sand. These are perfectly flush with the sand surface, numerous, and close together.

Animal burrows, on the other hand, generally show evidence of having been dug. There may be piles of excavated sand around the hole (often a color different from that of the surface sand) or there may be an elevated cone. In some cases you will see sunken conical holes, or actual bits of tubes sticking out above the surface. The shape of the hole itself has meaning, too. At first you will not know what animal hides beneath, so you should carefully study the hole and then excavate the animal.

Unfortunately, it is not easy to dig out a burrowing animal. Those close to the surface present no problem, but many others either live in long tubes that extend deep into the sand or can dig almost as fast as you can shovel. One of the fastest creatures is the razor clam, which has a long,

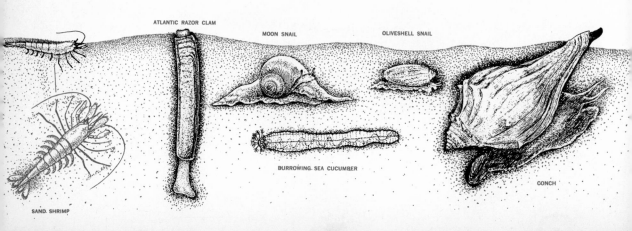

ATLANTIC RAZOR CLAM

MOON SNAIL

OLIVESHELL SNAIL

BURROWING SEA CUCUMBER

CONCH

SAND SHRIMP

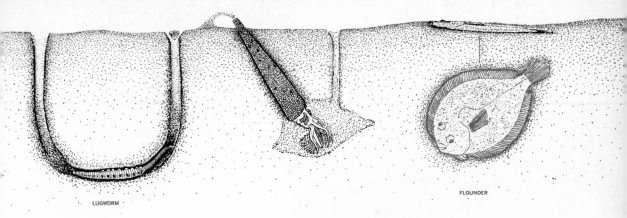

TRUMPET WORM

LUGWORM

FLOUNDER

muscular foot for digging. Its hole is a small, elongated oval opening without any sand piled around it. If you do not get a razor clam with the first or second shovelful, give up and try again elsewhere, for by then it is probably down in wet sand that caves in as you try to keep the hole open.

The plumed worm, which lives in a long parchmentlike tube, can sometimes be caught if you dig behind the tube very quickly. But you must grab it at once to keep it from escaping beyond your reach.

After you have had many failures in trying to collect burrowing animals, you will become wise to their ways of escape and to the peculiarities of their holes. Eventually you should be able to tell what lives in a particular stretch of beach merely by looking at the holes.

Some beach animals do not build burrows, but just live in the sand. To catch these, pour large samples of sand through a sieve. An ordinary kitchen strainer will do, but you can make a better sieve out of a wooden box with plastic window screening in place of the bottom. The dry sand of the upper beach, where insects and beach hoppers live, flows right through; the wet sand of the lower beach will have to be washed through with a trickle of water.

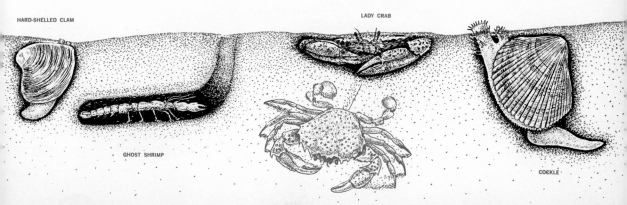

HARD-SHELLED CLAM

LADY CRAB

GHOST SHRIMP

COCKLE

CAPE COD NATIONAL SEASHORE

Long Point, the outermost tip of Cape Cod, arches like a beckoning finger into the sheltered waters of Cape Cod Bay. Only at low tide are the isolated beaches of this narrow sandbar accessible overland.

Formed by ancient glaciers, then molded by wind, waves, and ocean currents, the Cape Cod peninsula thrusts into the Atlantic from the Massachusetts coast. Long a haven for mariners, the isolated beaches of the outer Cape now accommodate thousands of summer vacationers seeking recreation and refreshment. In some places tall windswept bluffs overlook the roaring surf and the distant horizon of the Atlantic. Elsewhere, glistening dunes slope gently toward broad sandy beaches that extend for miles along the coast. Great salt marshes and tidal flats attract wheeling flocks of birds. Pine forests and areas of brushy heathland, picturesque villages, fresh-water ponds, and small secluded marshes all contribute to the varied beauties of the landscape. Although this National Seashore has not yet been fully developed, marked trails, lecture programs, and naturalist-guided tours are available for those who seek fuller understanding of the plants and animals of the shore. Ultimately it will embrace more than 25,000 acres set aside for the continuing enjoyment of all the people.

Rippled dunes yield constantly to the powers of the wind. In some places on Cape Cod, shifting dunes are gradually engulfing entire forests.

Life on the upper beach

You have already seen that the dry upper beach differs greatly from the moist intertidal region. Living things in one area will therefore be different from those in the other. If you look in the beach wrack and sift through the dried algae, bits of sponge, driftwood, and the like, you can find many small animals that most beach visitors never see: swift tiger beetles, sand-colored chrysomelid beetles, tiny springtails, weevils, fly maggots, and sexton beetles (in dead fish or clams). There also may be flies, burrowing mole crickets, earwigs under boards, and many other insects. One small predatory beetle that burrows in the sand beneath the wrack carries the name *hemispherical savage beetle*, which is a good deal longer than the insect itself. There are other joint-footed animals: flattened centipedes, slow-moving millipedes, and false scorpions that are like the poisonous scorpion of the deserts but smaller and without the stinging tail.

If you can catch a ghost crab above the wrack, examine it closely. Note that its legs are no longer useful for swimming. It is one of those fascinating animals in the process of changing from life in the water to life on the land. As an adult it cannot swim and does not enter water. It usually tries to avoid the sea, but is bound to the water because it breathes through gills that must be kept moist with sea water—from time to time it must go to the sea to fill its gill chambers. Ghost crabs also have to liberate their young into water as members of the plankton. Some other crustaceans, however, have entirely escaped the sea by breathing air and developing brood pouches in which they carry their larvae. These creatures include beach hoppers and certain isopods, such as the pillbugs, which you can find inland beneath logs and rocks.

Wedge-shaped coquina clams are sometimes incredibly abundant in the intertidal sand. Their delicate shells, less than an inch long, are so variable in coloration that it is difficult to find two exactly alike.

Animals of the intertidal sand

Moving down from the dry upper part of the beach into the wet intertidal region, you can continue to apply the techniques of watching tracks, seeking burrows, digging, and sifting the sand through the sieve.

You may not find many different kinds of animals on a particular beach, but the number of individual animals can be spectacular. Along southern beaches of both coasts, the sand may be alive with small active clams, the coquinas

78

(*Donax*). Like the mole crab, these brightly colored little bivalves rise out of the sand to allow the waves to wash them up and down the beach with each change of tide, after which they dig into the sand again. Hundreds or thousands of coquinas cluster in certain parts of a beach where the feeding is good. When they erupt from the sand, the shoreline sparkles with reflections from their shells.

Beach populations of other species can also be astonishingly large. Three million clams were removed by diggers in two months along one California beach four miles long. No one knows what part of the total population this was, but it cannot have been all. On a similar California beach, biologists estimated that in a strip one mile long, ten feet wide, and a foot deep there were nearly 160 million worms of a particular kind.

Instead of living in vast populations, some animals may appear as relatively isolated individuals. Beach hoppers that are numerous enough on the upper beach to make clouds as they jump into the air are represented by a more isolated relative closer to the water, the burrowing amphipod, *Haustorius*. It feeds upon organic matter several inches below the surface. Clams, in addition to the coquinas, include gapers, ark shells, cockles, hard clams, razor clams, tellins, and others which live in the lower intertidal zone on both coasts. The variety of burrowing worms is also large: trumpet worms in their sandy cases, parchment worms in long U-shaped tubes, beak-throwers, sandworms (nereids), cirratulids (fringed worms) with their long tentacles, stout lugworms (lobworms), and ribbon worms, to name but a few.

Here photographed in a glass tube is the front half of a parchment worm. By pumping a steady current of water through its U-shaped parchment-lined tube, the six-inch-long worm receives a constant supply of food and oxygen. At the left is a tiny crab that often shares the worm's home and food supply.

Animals below low tide

On down the beach to the lowest part of the intertidal region and in the region immediately below the low-tide mark, you can find burrowing sea cucumbers, flat sand dollars, burrowing sand shrimps, ghost shrimps in their tunnels, young flounders, gobies, cusk eels, clams, burrowing sea anemones, and a multitude of other creatures that cannot stand exposure to air and sunlight.

Farther below the low-tide mark is the longshore trough, a region of great turbulence and a dangerous place to live. It is largely barren. Beyond may be a sand bar, however, which at low tide is a fertile collecting ground for creatures that live buried in the sand. Large numbers of crabs usually either lurk here partly buried or walk across the sand hunting for food.

Try to find some crustaceans in the sand below the low-tide mark and note which way they face. They are turned toward the shore, not the sea. Why? Remember the way the water rushes up the beach and how it returns as backwash, continuing out across the bottom as undertow? Surface plankton from the sea flows up and back with the bottom currents, which also carry organic matter washed down from the beach itself. Thus the crustaceans facing the beach get food from two sources instead of one.

By now, if you have kept a list of what animals you found on a cross-section of the beach, you have some idea of zonation in the intertidal region. Along the Atlantic beaches, for example, the order from the shore out into the water for crustaceans alone generally is sand crab, mole crab, lady crab, box crab, sand shrimp, and blue crab. Similar patterns exist along the Pacific shore, but the species are different.

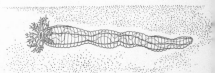

BURROWING SEA CUCUMBER

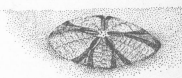

SAND DOLLAR

Survival in the sand

Although vast numbers of animals often live in a beach, it seems a hostile, precarious environment compared with other shorelines. Because strong waves can expose and kill, many

Frilled with showy pink gills, the foot-long plumed worm emerges partway from its three-foot parchment tube in the sand and gropes for food in the surrounding water. The top of the tube, which projects about three inches from the bottom just below low tide, is decorated with bits of shell and seaweed.

81

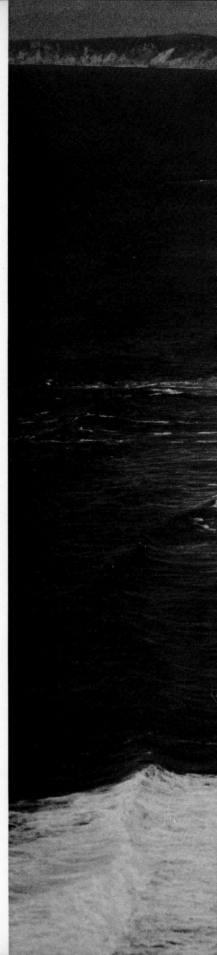

Point Reyes, a massive peninsula on the California
coast, is a magnificent gateway to the sea. From the
forested summit of Inverness Ridge, near the
mainland, the undulating landscape of hills and
valleys merges with a distant ocean panorama.
Although this National Seashore includes only part
of the peninsula, owners of much of the remaining
acreage have agreed to maintain their land as farms
and ranches and thus preserve the pastoral
atmosphere of this secluded outpost on the Pacific.
The prime attraction here is the sea itself with its
broad uncluttered beaches that encircle the
peninsula. Battering the headlands incessantly,
waves have carved the rocks into craggy palisades
that extend for miles along the coast. In sheltered
areas, the shoreline is indented by tranquil bays and
lagoons which are enclosed by shifting dunes and
grassy lowlands. Special attractions at Point Reyes
include large colonies of sea birds that congregate
on offshore rocks and a herd of sea lions that
frequents part of the coast. Opportunities for
swimming, fishing, hiking, and picnicking also lure
a steady stream of visitors from nearby cities.

*From the distant reaches of
the Pacific, waves surge in
and bathe the coast of Point
Reyes National Seashore with
foaming surf. Along much of
the coast, a rugged backdrop
of tall jagged cliffs creates a
dramatic seascape.*

beach animals must burrow rapidly. Animals that live deep in the sand must avoid suffocation. These creatures are adapted to life under the sand; they block gill openings to keep out sand particles, or vigorously pump water to get in more oxygen, or increase their gill area to get the most benefit from oxygen-poor water.

Clams and snails living in sand are streamlined for rapid digging or efficient creeping through the loose particles. The slender razor clam is an example of a rapid digger, while the oliveshell snail creeps through the sand, feeding on organic matter. Poor vision, or no vision at all, in many sand dwellers does not lessen their chances of survival. Instead of sight, many sand animals have highly developed means of sensing water movement, so they can follow or escape from the water, depending on their needs.

Despite their adaptations, many beach animals do die when large volumes of sand are washed away in violent storms. In addition, at times of extreme tides when the sand is exposed to the sun for a long time, animals close to the surface may die from prolonged high temperatures.

The beach is more thickly populated with larger, or visible, animals than it at first appears to be. Even so, it is not a favorable place in which to live. Though many individuals die from extreme conditions, the reproduction rate is often high, and huge populations result. It is important to remember that shore conditions are extreme. Beach life must not only adapt to normal waves and tides but survive, if possible, sudden storms which shift the sand violently and actually alter the contours of the beach itself, thus even changing the flow of currents.

Most of its relatives must cling to rocks and other hard surfaces, but the burrowing anemone thrives on sandy and muddy bottoms. Anchored in place by a slender, tapering body, only the crown of tentacles projects above the sand.

Life between the sand grains

There is yet another world of the intertidal beach invisible to the unaided eye. It includes practically the only plants of the beach and a variety of microscopic animals.

Microscopic dinoflagellates resembling bits of lichen on boulders navigate through the pore spaces between sand grains. Dinoflagellates can move about like animals, yet like plants they manufacture food through photosynthesis. Sometimes they are so abundant in the lower intertidal sand that they color it a yellowish-brown.

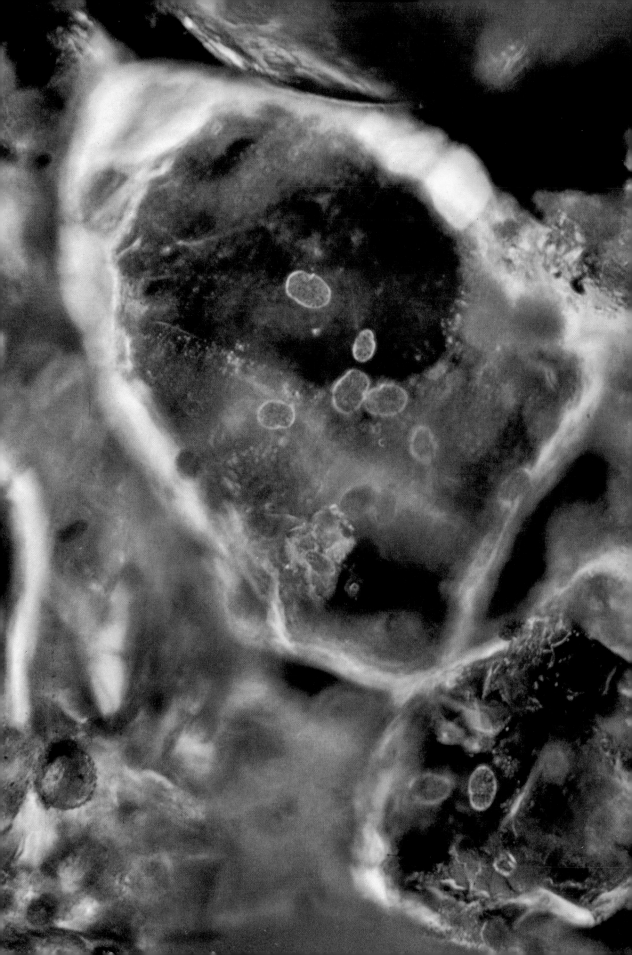

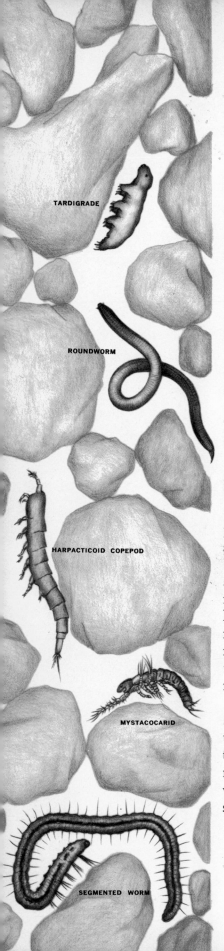

TARDIGRADE

ROUNDWORM

HARPACTICOID COPEPOD

MYSTACOCARID

SEGMENTED WORM

The plants must be viewed at a magnification of at least 100 diameters; they are most likely to be diatoms, which have pleasing, geometric shapes, and the active, oval plant-animals known as dinoflagellates. The latter have *flagella*, whiplike hairs, with which they swim about in the film between grains of sand. At times either or both of these photosynthetic organisms may be so numerous as to color the wet sand of the lower intertidal region a yellowish-brown.

The smallest of the microscopic beach animals are the protozoans, relatives of the familiar fresh-water *Amoeba* and *Paramecium*. Some crawl over each sand grain with "legs" formed by a number of hairlike cilia fused together. Others swim through the water film between sand grains. Some are rather long, but all are exceedingly slender so they can slip between sand grains easily.

At times in a cubic inch of wet sand you can find thousands of roundworms. Other creatures adapted to life among the grains are the harpacticoid copepods, small crustaceans of the same major group as much of the sea's plankton. These animals have well-developed legs for crawling through the sand.

Some of the animals and most of the plants that live among the sand grains rise and fall beneath the surface of the beach according to the tides. The plants have to be close to the wet surface at low tide to get sunlight for photosynthesis. The animals, on the other hand, come to the sand surface at flood tide to find food.

The microscopic world is more extensive than you might suspect. Although sand grains touch one another, there are many spaces between their irregular shapes. This pore space holds water and leaves plenty of room for small animals to move about. For a given volume of sand, only 80 per cent is really sand; 20 per cent is space. When filled with sea water, this space provides an almost limitless environment for minute life.

For these tiny organisms, conditions in the sand are quite stable. The sand protects them from extreme changes of temperature and salt, even after prolonged sunlight at low tide has heated and dried the sand above. Floods of fresh rainwater likewise have little effect on the subsurface environment. Hence the sand–water environment is always salty and cool.

86

The sand itself

In sifting the dry sand to find life, you will probably notice that the particles above the high-tide mark are the coarsest (largest) and that the grains become smaller as you go nearer the water. Wind has carried the powdery dry sand away to form a barrier dune, leaving the coarser grains behind. Underwater, waves also sort sand grains, depositing the finest in the intertidal zone and leaving coarser sand farther out to sea.

Where does all the sand come from? It was brought up by currents and tides from the continental shelf and deposited on the beach by waves. But originally the sand was carried from land down to the sea by rivers. Throughout most of North America, the erosion of granite or granite-type rocks has produced quartz sand. On some southern and many tropical beaches, however, sand is a limy or calcareous material composed of broken-down shells, corals, and the substances left by lime-depositing algae. Quartz sand is likely to be fine, hard-packed, with somewhat rounded grains that make a much better home for living things than the coarse, loosely packed calcareous sand with its sharp, irregular edges and tendency to crumble.

The zonation of rocky shores

It takes careful observation to see most of the zonation on a beach. But the zonation of the steep, rocky shore stands out clearly from a distance. The best time to observe it is at low tide during the greatest tides of a lunar month. Even

A variety of animals and plants is shown in this highly generalized diagram. Zonation patterns on shoreline rocks are the result of several factors, one being the ability of an organism to survive exposure during low tide. Closely related forms of life may be separated. For example, two different species of barnacles are shown here: *Chthamalus* in the upper intertidal and *Balanus* in the lower intertidal region.

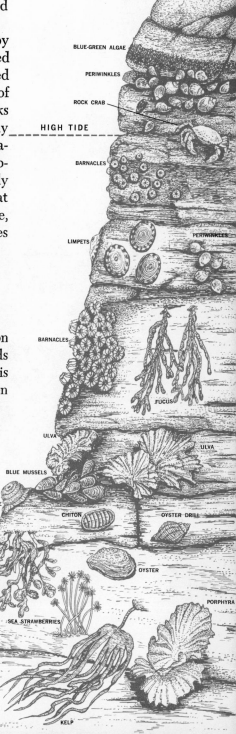

The rocky inlets and tide pools of Point Lobos State Reserve in Monterey County, California, harbor a great variety of marine plants and animals. The area gets its name from barking sea lions that bask on the rocks at Punta de los Lobos Marinos (Point of the Seawolves). The Reserve is the home of two species of sea lions and is the northernmost breeding ground of the California brown pelican. Sea otters and gray whales as well as cormorants, gulls, and other waterfowl can be seen at times from the rocky cliffs upon which cling groves of the rare Monterey cypress.

from far away, you can see quite clearly the various horizontal bands of colored seaweeds. Bare rock is at the top, then green, brown, and possibly a purplish-red seaweed lowest, awash in the surf. Here and there on the lower rocks you may also see spots or lines of white and black. The white is probably barnacles and the black mussels.

Close-up, of course, the boundaries of the zones on the rocky shore are not so distinct. For example, holes and crevices in the rocks disrupt the patterns. In such spots, waves do not beat so hard, temperature changes less, and water evaporates more slowly from the rocks. Because the crevices remain cool, dark, and wet, some fragile animals, such as hydroids, bryozoans, and the flowerlike sea anemones, do well here above their normal zone.

Above the high-tide mark

Now go to the top of a rocky shore and climb down. In an area well above the highest tide mark you may find either dark, grayish lichens or bright orange ones. Spray or the splash of waves sometimes wets this region during high tide, but lichens are probably the toughest plants in the world and can stand extreme conditions of light, temperature, and—in this case—salt water. Lichens usually colonize rock above the water line before any other plant. The growth is really a remarkable combination of two different plants, an alga held in the filaments of a fungus. Some experts believe this strange partnership benefits both, but others think the fungus is a parasite on the alga.

On the rocks below the lichens is a rather surprising plant for this location: a green alga of a type also found in the wet intertidal region. This slender, hollow, threadlike plant,

Midge larva zone

Enteromorpha zone

Barnacle (Balanus) and rockweed zone

Ulva zone

Water line

Mussel zone

TWO EXAMPLES OF ROCKY SHORE ZONATION

On the left, a Middle Atlantic artificial rocky shore (exposed breakwater); on the right, a New England rocky shore (protected shoreline).

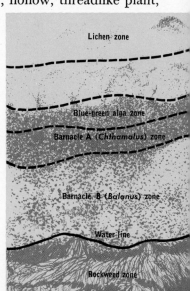

Lichen zone

Blue-green alga zone

Barnacle A (Chthamalus) zone

Barnacle B (Balanus) zone

Water line

Rockweed zone

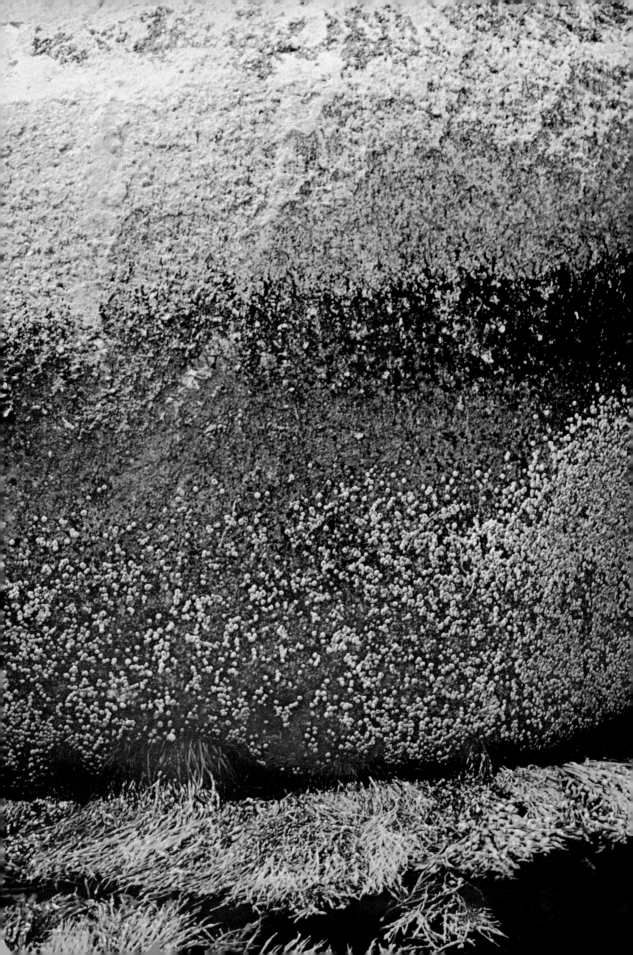

Various species of periwinkles range from the intertidal region to the splash zone above high tide on rocky coasts throughout the world. These small snails use their rasplike tongues to scrape microscopic algae from the surface as they creep across the rocks. The large yellow seaweed at the lower right is a brown alga (*Ascophyllum*).

known as sea hair, or *Enteromorpha,* can live wherever moisture is thrown against the rocks as spray. Although most algae quickly dry out and die when exposed to sun for any length of time, *Enteromorpha* can survive on a minimum of moisture. Here also can be a dark band of microscopic blue-green algae, almost black in their total effect.

In the same region above the highest tide mark, a number of insects are active. Some, such as springtails, flies, and beetles, can scurry or fly out of the way if high waves wash over their feeding grounds; others, such as midge larvae, live in tubes cemented against the rock and at times are soaked with splashing sea water or even completely submerged at high tide.

Whereas insects are chiefly active during the day, at night you will find that crustaceans have taken over. Small isopods and agile crabs run across the rocks scavenging for bits of food, mostly *detritus* (the remains of plants and animals). Some crustaceans are fast-moving enough to capture such living prey as worms and even smaller shrimplike animals.

The intertidal region

A little farther down the rocks in the intertidal region, you will see clearly defined zones of both plants and animals. The seaweeds are usually rockweeds (*Fucus*), brownish-green algae that often have small air bladders at the ends of their fronds. Each species of fucoid alga lives in its own zone, which you should be able to distinguish. A little farther down, but still fairly high in the intertidal region, you will find emerald-green sea lettuce, *Ulva*, with its thin, wide, wrinkled fronds.

Among the fronds of seaweeds from the upper intertidal region you will find periwinkles, limpets, and small crustaceans.

The periwinkle lives throughout the world. Each of our coasts has half a dozen species; most of these live in particular areas. Light-colored varieties prefer lighted regions and darker ones occupy shadowy crevices. Some species

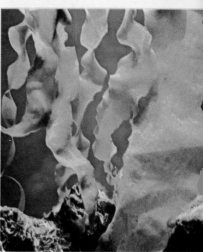

Two algae common on rocky coasts are *Ulva,* or sea lettuce (*top*), and *Laminaria,* one of the kelps (*bottom*).

The calm waters of a sheltered cove belie the power of the sea, the force that carved the rugged beauty of this coast. Yet even the pebbles on the beach were milled from rocks torn from the surrounding cliffs.

The lower rocks of an Acadian cliff, alternately covered by sea and exposed to air, are marked by horizontal bands of color. Each zone is inhabited by a different community of plants and animals.

ACADIA NATIONAL PARK

Acadia National Park on the coast of Maine includes parts of Mount Desert Island and Isle au Haut, part of Schoodic Peninsula, and several smaller islands. Pounding against the cliffs for centuries, waves have dislodged great blocks of granite. At Anemone Cave the pounding surf has gnawed a cavern 82 feet into solid rock. Elsewhere gigantic rocks lie heaped along the beach like natural sea walls. In contrast are the many peaceful coves and harbors that dot the shoreline.

Although sea birds—gulls, guillemots, ducks, and others—are always present at Acadia, the wealth of life on this magnificent coast is best revealed at low tide. Draped with seaweeds and studded with barnacles, the intertidal rocks then emerge like miniature islands from a maze of tide pools. The pools contain a variety of living things— seaweeds, sea stars, periwinkles, anemones, sea urchins, and crabs— each adapted in its own way to life along the turbulent boundary between land and sea.

On the coast of Maine, where conifers grow close to the shore, low tide reveals the tangled beds of seaweed that covers the rocks.

stay very high in the intertidal region, even in the splash zone, and feed at low tide. Others much nearer the low-tide mark feed only when covered with water. Periwinkles move up and down within their zones during the lunar month with the increase and decrease in the maximum height of high tide. During storms periwinkles may migrate to higher levels. Their different abilities to withstand exposure to air seems to govern how high each species will climb. The distinct living zones enable the various species to avoid too much competition with one another.

On the rocky shore, the middle of the intertidal region, which is alternately covered and uncovered by the tides, is known as the *barnacle zone,* although not all barnacles live there. Acorn barnacles are especially numerous. They may all look alike, but experts can distinguish many distinct species. You can find some differences if you remove a few barnacles from the rocks. One major difference is in the baseplate, which can be white and calcareous (stony) or brownish and membranous (leathery). One of the common barnacles with a membranous base, *Chthamalus fragilis,* lives in the upper half of the intertidal region. Another, with a calcareous base, *Balanus eburneus,* lives in the lower intertidal region. These two animals, so much alike in appearance and way of life, live permanently separated from each other.

Past the midpoint of the intertidal region going toward the sea is a greater profusion of plant and animal life. After all, most of these organisms are originally from the sea and they can live in the intertidal region only to the extent that

they can stand exposure to air and light. The closer these plants and animals are to the water, the less time they have to spend exposed.

Rockweeds begin to give way to other brown algae, the *kelps* or *laminarians*. Close to the lowest zone and extending out into the sea, red algae become common. Kelp are large, straplike plants with strong holdfasts, and in some areas in shallow water off the California coast kelp forms dense forests of great flat ribbons swaying in the surge of the waves. These can be dangerous to a skindiver who becomes lost or caught in their tangled masses. Red algae, on the other hand, are usually delicate and small. If you float some of these onto a paper mount, you will be surprised how little substance they possess. When dry they leave only a fine tracery of plant tissue upon the paper.

You can find a large variety of animals living among the plants low on a rocky shore. They include delicate hydroids, large sea anemones, tubeworms, bryozoans, mussels, and oysters—all attached forms. Mobile animals, among others, are long-legged spider crabs, hermit crabs wearing snail-shells, various snails, five-armed sea stars, spiny sea urchins, and pop-eyed gobies. This zone is the most heavily populated of the intertidal region.

Such heavy populations bring on a housing shortage, sometimes with startling effects. Take barnacles, for example. Those that are higher on the rocks live separated from one another and are conical with round or oval bases. In the crowded lower regions, where they are packed together per-

After the tide has covered them, barnacles sweep plankton and detritus from the water with their feathery legs, then comb the food into their mouths *(this page)*. When falling tide exposes them to the air *(next page)*, each barnacle closes the valves at the top of its shell to form a snug, moist chamber. Among the most bizarre of crustaceans, barnacles are free-swimming, shrimplike forms in their larval stages. Later they settle on rocks, boats, and other surfaces and secrete a permanently attached shell of limy plates. As the surface becomes overcrowded *(facing next page)*, the shells of the older barnacles elongate and eventually are undercut by the growth of younger barnacles.

haps 4000 to a square foot, they are as tall and narrow as masses of pipes pressed together. Each must grow this way to reach the water and cannot spread out because of pressure from neighbors.

If you count the population of small, young mussels on an exposed rock in the spring after a particularly heavy "set," then count them again late in the summer, you will find that the mortality rate is astounding. Possibly 97 per cent have disappeared. Predators and waves take their toll, to be sure, but more than anything else, lack of space in which to grow kills off most of the mussels. The same space is still completely occupied by mussels, but there are fewer of them because they have grown so much.

BLUE MUSSELS

OYSTER DRILL

Two worlds

Although the intertidal region is a single environment, you can observe two different patterns of activity among the animals there. During the highest tides of the month observation is difficult. The water is turbid, and visibility, even if you wear a mask and snorkle, is poor. If you can see the bottom, however, you may find great activity. Animals that were quiet at low tide are now active. Newcomers have invaded the region from the sea.

Scuttling over the bottom may be hordes of hermit crabs, those peculiar small crustaceans that pick up empty snail-shells to live in. Close by will be swimming crabs, usually buried in sand except for their eyes and antennae, sharp claws poised just beneath the surface ready to strike. Equally hard to see are the digging fish: flounders and skates with only their eyes and gill openings showing, and cusk eels and gobies, which dig more deeply, some excavating burrows. Such swimming fish as silversides, anchovies, and killifish dart through the shallow water.

In shallow coastal water, schools of two- to three-inch-long fish known as silversides often glitter with reflected sunlight. This one hovers over a tuft of red alga.

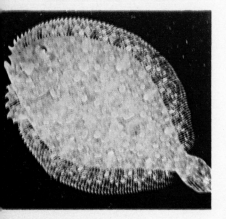

When the tides cover such harder bottoms as rocks and pilings, attached animals become active immediately, for this is the only time they can feed. Even in a small area, thousands of barnacles vigorously whip their feathery legs in and out, sifting plankton that comes their way. Huge populations of small bottom-dwelling crustaceans emerge to browse in the same area. A caprellid, or skeleton shrimp, stands erect on hind legs and waves its long body about in the water, occasionally reaching out with powerful sickle-shaped claws to snag a passing worm or crustacean. These shrimp look like miniature boxers feinting with heavy gloves.

Snails and limpets leave their secure home bases to browse, scraping off diatoms and other plants with rasplike tongues. The tongue, known as a *radula*, resembles a flexible file and that of some species can actually rasp a hole, with the help of a chemical secretion, through the shell of an attached mollusc. In the beach wrack you can find clam shells with perfectly round little holes near the hinge, the work of predatory snails.

Most effective of all in their feeding habits are probably the bivalve molluscs of the intertidal region—mussels, clams, and oysters. As soon as the water covers them, they begin to filter out food and remove huge quantities in the few hours they are able to feed.

Some intertidal animals drown when the tide comes in. Many of these are insects, which must crawl, fly, or hop to higher ground. A few shoreline insects have special air sacs that provide air for a time if they are submerged. Long hairs on others trap air about their bodies. Some secrete wax that keeps water from wetting them. Such measures help the animals survive for a time, giving them a chance to reach safety.

A few of the crustaceans, like the insects, drown. Ghost crabs, which usually live in burrows above the high-tide mark, have to get out of the water if the tide catches them. Beach hoppers also must retreat to dry land.

When the tide goes out, the beach becomes quite another world. Now the invaders come from land, not sea. Birds

Poised above a bed of feeding barnacles, a caprellid shrimp clings to a support with short, hooked legs at the rear of its body. This unusual amphipod crustacean hunts by snatching small animals as they swim by, and by doubling over to capture worms and other animals that crawl on the surface below.

OLYMPIC NATIONAL PARK

Most famous for its rugged mountain wilderness and luxuriant rain forest, Olympic National Park in the state of Washington also includes one of the most beautiful seacoasts in the United States. Rocky cliffs rise abruptly from the Pacific; sheltered coves indent the shore; acres of tide pools glisten among the rocks. Offshore, islands and chimneylike seastacks jut from the water like fortresses. Seals, sea birds, and a multitude of smaller creatures share the coast with deer, bears, and other animals that frequently emerge from forests beside the sea. Although a highway traverses part of the narrow fifty-mile coastal area of the Park, the more remote sections of this scenic shoreline are reserved for those who travel on foot across the jagged headlands.

Conifers fringe the rocky
headlands of the Olympic
coast. Frequent fog and
heavy rainfall support
luxuriant forests in the inland
portions of the Park.

Seastacks, shiplike rocks that
dot the water along the
Olympic coast, provide
refuge for myriads of birds.
Seals also are a common
sight in the water and on the
offshore rocks.

This rock in Nauset Marsh, Cape Cod, is visited frequently by gulls. Hovering fifteen to twenty feet overhead, the gulls drop clams and mussels on the rock, then descend to pick the flesh from the shattered shells.

probe deeply into sand and mud, turn over bits of wood and stone, and hunt through seaweed. Their prey—molluscs, crustaceans, and worms—are hiding in these places. If you lie on the crest of a barrier dune or watch from a high rock, you can observe the feeding activities of birds. Binoculars will help you make out what they capture. If you cannot tell, note the spot where they feed and later you may be able to find the remains of the meal. In this way you can sometimes detect the presence of certain animals you might not have known about.

On some shores you can watch the clean dive of a tern, which may emerge from the water with a small fish. In the Florida Keys, big brown pelicans dive less gracefully, capturing fish with their bills and carrying their catch in their great pouches. Black skimmers cleave the water with their bills as they fly close to the shore, snapping up fish. On every shore noisy gulls fight and clamor over bits of food, dead and alive. You may see a gull pick up a clam or mussel, fly high over a rocky ledge, and drop it to the rocks below, where it shatters. The gull then swoops down, lands, and eats the exposed flesh.

With an old fishhead on a string you can attract hungry blue crabs along the Middle Atlantic coast. Sea stars nearby send scallops, limpets, hermit crabs, and even sea anemones into frenzied escape maneuvers. If you are snorkling in clear shallow water, you may see a flat, broad skate glide over the bottom, stop, and with an enormous gulp lift a whole razor clam out of the sand with suction alone.

It is plain that one of the major activities of all seashore animals is feeding. Usually there seems to be enough food for all the many different kinds of inhabitants, but apparently they must eat at every opportunity if they are to survive.

For many of the plants and creatures, however, there is another important task when the tide retreats—to avoid drying out. Although seaweeds are not protected from water loss as land plants are, they conserve water so well by massing together that animals can find shelter and moisture among them. On rocky shores, shelled animals hug the stones; certain limpets even make a watertight seal by fitting the edges of their shells carefully into a ring they and their predecessors have cut into the rock after years of returning to the same spot at low tide. The creatures of the intertidal region are able to survive in the air for much longer than they usually have to. Periwinkles taken from a rock can remain sealed up for days and will emerge once again, none the worse, when placed in water. Certain barnacles have survived forty-four days of exposure to air. Even sea anemones, soft-bodied and without shells, conserve water well enough if they are not exposed to direct sunlight.

Sea worlds in miniature

Along rocky and coral shores, in breakwaters or perhaps in an old wreck, you will come across pools left by the retreating tide. When you find one, stop! Watching a tide pool is as interesting as walking for hours on the beach.

In the daytime, much of the activity in a tide pool will cease as you approach, for most of the animals see well enough to detect motion outside the water. You should lie down at the edge of the pool, perhaps shading the water to reduce reflections, and watch quietly. Before long, small animals will begin to move about.

The tide pool is fascinating because it is a miniature sea in some respects; in other ways it presents unique problems for its inhabitants. It is a place of refuge for a plant or animal that could not stand exposure to air during low tide, but

Temporarily isolated by the ebbing sea, tide pools shimmer among the rocks at Olympic National Park, Washington. In spite of their frequently high temperatures, oxygen shortages, and variable salt content, tide pools usually abound with colorful plants and animals.

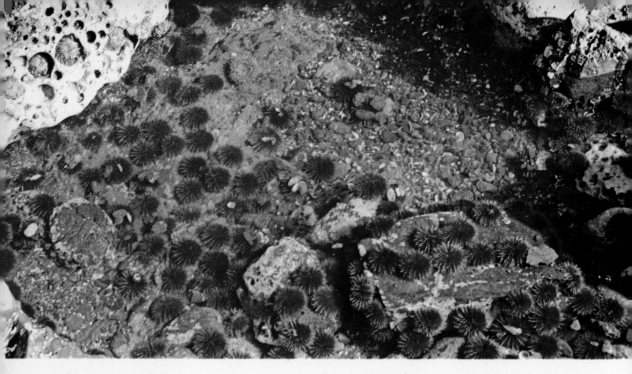

Sea urchins stud the bottom of this Pacific tide pool with bursts of color. With their long sucking tube feet, sea urchins can walk across the rock or anchor themselves firmly to the surface. As a further defense against the waves, they sometimes use their movable spines to brace themselves in holes and crevices among the rocks (*upper left*).

because it is small and isolated from the sea when the tide is out, the pool also may cause the death of marine animals. Sometimes they suffocate for lack of oxygen, and sometimes they have to cope with too much or too little salt in the water.

The tide pool is likely to be fairly permanent and hold water through each low tide. If so, green, brown, and red seaweeds may hang down the sides and carpet the bottom. From their hiding places in the algae, the pool's inhabitants will begin to appear—small fish, snails, sea stars, sea urchins, shrimps, crabs, worms, and perhaps even a little squid or two.

Since the animals are trapped in a small space, you can easily see how they interact with one another, which you could hardly do were they in the sea. Periwinkles rasp away fronds of seaweeds or remove diatoms from the rock surfaces. An oyster drill resting quietly on a mussel is actually drilling a hole into its shell so that it can get out the soft tissues. Small bottom-dwelling fish such as gobies sit almost motionless, inflating and emptying their gill chambers, until suddenly they gulp in a shrimp or worm that has wandered by. Then the goby falls victim to a quick-clawed crab that has waited in an even more motionless state. Sea anemones stretch out from the seaweeds to capture a worm or shrimp that blunders against the stinging tentacles. A sea star is wrapped around a mussel trying to open the shell against the powerful muscle of the bivalve. A nereid worm, creeping slowly over the bottom, shoots out its proboscis. The two curved sharp jaws at the end easily skewer a smaller animal. Oyster catchers and other birds of rocky shores visit tide pools. Oyster catchers have chisel-like bills which they use for separating the shells of bivalve molluscs.

You never know beforehand what you will find in a tide pool. Crawling over the algae may be a brightly colored, fantastically shaped sea slug, or *nudibranch.* Hydroid colonies may house a bizarre spindly sea spider, a creature with eight legs but not closely related to land spiders. Sponges and sea squirts—the former one of the simplest of all animals and the latter related to the most complex—exist side by side on the bottom. Both feed on the limited amount of plankton trapped in the pool. The roll call of tide-pool inhabitants is almost endless.

The perilous world of the tide pool

If a pool has been exposed to the hot sun for a few hours while the tide is out, you can see signs of distress among the animals. Watch for rapid gill movements of the fish and crustaceans. Some may be limp, others dead. Put your finger or a thermometer into the water and compare the temperature with that of the sea. The water might be as hot as 100° Fahrenheit under such conditions—hot enough to kill most marine animals.

It is not simply heat but also a lack of oxygen that threatens the animals. Under normal conditions enough oxygen from the air dissolves through the surface of the water, but as the water heats up oxygen is driven off. Animals that cannot close up in their shells to await a new supply of oxygen will gradually suffocate. On other parts of the shore, the problem does not arise, for beating waves mix enough oxygen into the water, even in warm tropic seas. Incidentally, you can also make observations on the oxygen problem outside a tide pool. Some crustaceans of the intertidal region have gills that vary in size depending upon the amount of oxygen available to them. Atlantic-coast crabs that live higher in the intertidal region have fewer and smaller gills than those living farther down. To see this, examine in turn a ghost crab, a purple marsh crab, a fiddler crab, the various mud crabs, a stone crab, and a blue crab.

At night in the tide pool it is cooler, yet the oxygen level

The peacock worm is a common inhabitant of tide pools. With only its head projecting from a parchmentlike tube, it takes food from water funneled into its mouth by a crown of feathery tentacles. Even a passing shadow causes the peacock worm to withdraw like a flash into its tube.

109

could still fall dangerously low. Without sunlight plants cannot carry on photosynthesis, giving off oxygen and taking in carbon dioxide as they do in the daytime. They can only do what animals do all the time—take in oxygen and release carbon dioxide. Hence the animals can suffocate at night even without excessive heat. But if a pool is shallow and covers a large area, enough oxygen from the air dissolves through the surface to keep most of the animals and plants alive.

There is still another problem for life in a tide pool. On a hot, dry day, look around the margins of a pool for a white crust. If you find one, taste it. After long exposure to the sun since the last high tide, some of the water evaporates, leaving salt around the rim. Evaporation also means there is more salt in the remaining water than is normal for the sea, which makes it difficult for many of the marine animals to survive. A heavy rain, on the other hand, dilutes the salt in a tide pool, and can be an even more serious problem.

Sea water contains about thirty parts of salt to a thousand parts of water and thus is approximately 97 per cent water.

A sea star wraps its body around a mussel (*left*), then pulls the valves slowly apart with its powerful sucking tube feet (*right*). Once the shell has been opened, the sea star everts its stomach through its mouth, wraps it around the mussel's fleshy body, and digests its prey.

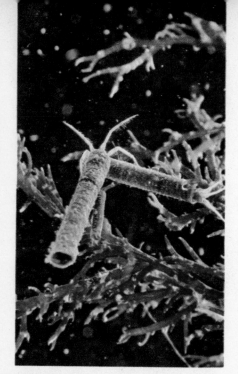

By flipping the two pairs of antennae that protrude from its neatly built tube of plant debris, a tube-dwelling shrimp can swim with a rapid jerking motion. These minute amphipods often abound among the seaweed in tide pools.

As this sea slug creeps across the bottom or over green algae, its crinkled mantle may either be extended as shown here or folded over its back.

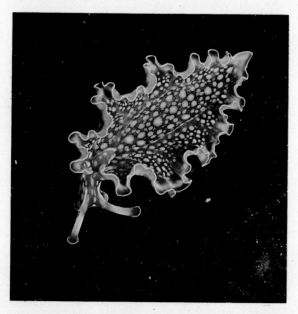

Fresh water, however, is nearly 100 per cent water (most fresh water, except rainwater, does contain an extremely small amount of salt). The difference between fresh and salt water is extremely important to animals that must maintain a sensitive balance of water and salts in their body fluids. The blood, or body fluid, of most marine animals has about as much salt as the sea. The blood of man and many other land animals contains less salt but does have about the same proportions of the minerals of which the salts are composed. Sea animals that find themselves in less salty water lose the essential balance between water and salts. The excess of water in a less salty environment seeps into their tissues and inflates the animals, causing them to swell up and die. In a tide pool, the soft-bodied sea slugs, sea anemones, and hydroids suffer inflation after a heavy rain. When the water is saltier than that of the sea many animals lose internal fluid to the water around them, a condition which also may be deadly.

Fresh-water and land animals with blood like that of sea animals have efficient organs to bail out the fluid coming

112

into their tissues, either from the surrounding water or from water they drink. These bailing organs are kidneys, which fresh-water fish possess, as does man. (In general, the kidneys of marine animals are relatively undeveloped.) There are very few fresh-water animals that can enter the ocean, for they lose fluid when they are in sea water. Only those animals with watertight skins, such as muskrats, seals, sea lions, sea otters, and man, as well as turtles, various sea birds, and certain insects can survive in salt water.

Some fish are famous for their migrations, for purposes of reproduction, between the sea and fresh water. Salmon, eel, shad, and others undergo complicated changes in body chemistry that force them to seek water of a different kind. They migrate only because they have to. Few animals of the marine world can penetrate rivers, but some that do include the blue crab of the East Coast, certain members of the herring family, a small flounder known as a hogchoker, and a small transparent shrimp (*Palaemonetes*).

On legs that span scarcely half an inch this sea spider clambers easily through the tangled branches of hydroid colonies and seaweeds. These unusual animals are only distant relatives of land spiders.

Instead of swimming freely
through the water like most
of its relatives, the colorful
clown jellyfish—about an inch
in diameter and an inch high—
lives attached to plants, rocks,
and other objects beneath
the water; the stalk projecting
from the center of its
trumpet-shaped body is
equipped with an adhesive
clinging pad. The smaller knobs
that hang from the perimeter
of the body are also
gripping pads. To move from
place to place, the jellyfish clings
alternately with one or two
of these and with the large
central stalk, inching forward
measuring-worm fashion.

The large reddish structures
within the clown's bell-shaped
body are reproductive organs,
and the eight sunburstlike
pompons around the edge are
clusters of stinging tentacles.
The clown jellyfish captures
such passing prey as caprellid
shrimp by stinging them and
then folding both the cluster
of tentacles and the paralyzed
victim down to the mouth
(not visible in this picture)
at the center of the funnel-like
body.

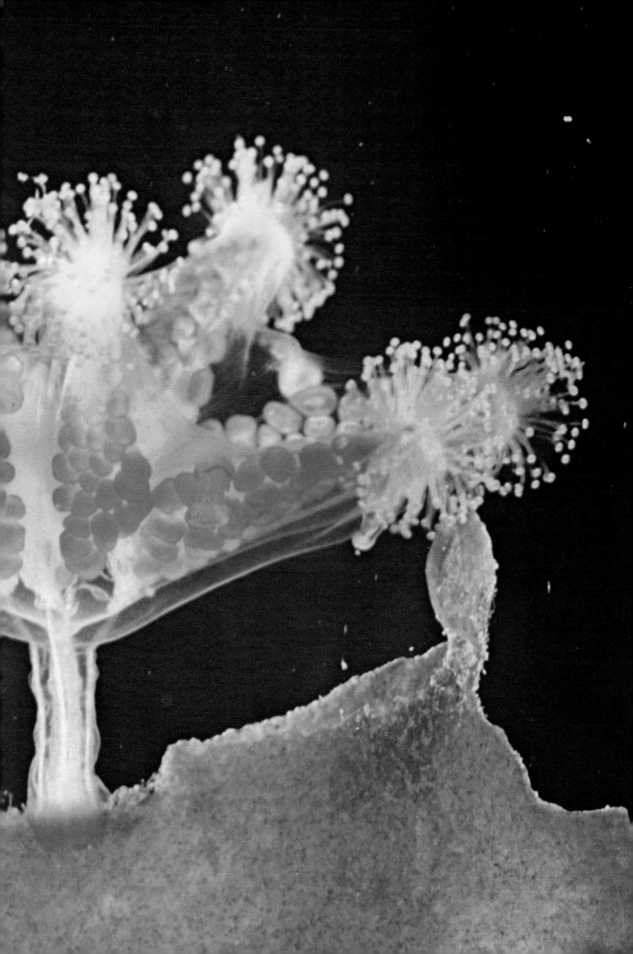

Below the tides

The world beneath the low-tide mark on both rocky and sandy shores is a brief continuation of the lower intertidal region. On a rocky shore, remember to search for a quiet spot where you can look with a face mask or a glass-bottom bucket.

Depending on the shoreline you visit, a glimpse underwater along a rocky shore will reveal so much you can't take it all in—long ribbons of kelp, forests of rockweed, clusters of red algae, dense beds of mussels, bunches of sea squirts, goose barnacles, corals of all shapes and colors, and sponges. You may see lobsters, big crabs, octopus, darting squid, and, of course, everywhere you look many kinds of fish. Hundreds of writers have described the colorful scenes of this underwater world, and it is all true. You cannot imagine it; you must see for yourself, and then you will want to join the thousands of others who wish to enter this world of water and explore it.

If you could follow the bottom out toward the edge of

Among the simplest of animals, sponges extract food from streams of water that they draw in through pores. Despite their basic simplicity, sponges occur in a bewildering variety of forms and colors in the world below low tide. Several different kinds are visible in this picture.

the continental shelf, you would find seaweeds growing scarce and then disappearing, for not enough sunlight can reach them. At depths of fifty feet nearly all of them are gone.

Offshore, distinct zones of animal life are difficult to notice. The different populations in different places along the continental shelf seem to be the result of variations in the bottom sediment rather than the result of the distance from shore. Where a river empties into the sea, the sediments are thicker and the animals quite different from those in clear water with a sandy bottom.

It is difficult to examine the populations of a continental shelf unless you are studying marine biology professionally. Taking samples requires dredging from a research vessel or extensive scuba diving.

Three anemonelike zoanthids flare like morning-glories in an underwater garden of sponges, corals, and other animals and plants. This zoanthid, a West Indian species sometimes also found in Florida waters, often grows in colonies of as many as fifty or sixty individual polyps.

Tidal flats and marshes

Another, entirely different type of shoreline world is the tidal flat and the somewhat similar tidal marsh at its edge. Neither a clean, sandy beach nor a high, rocky cliff with waves surging against it, the tidal flat is a vast, shallow mud flat, usually surrounded by marsh that is densely covered

117

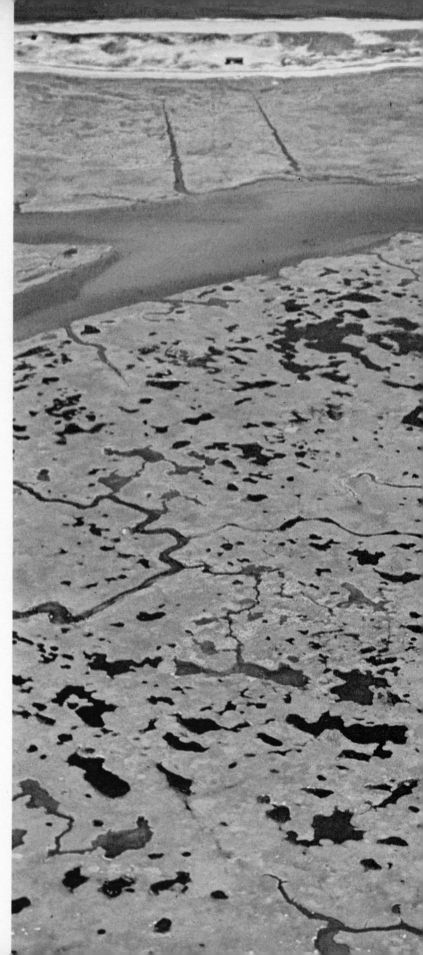

Nauset Marsh, now included within Cape Cod National Seashore, is a prime example of an East Coast marsh. Protected from the heavy surf by the dunes of Nauset Beach (*top*), the marsh includes enormous tidal flats across which great sheets of water slip quietly back and forth as the tide rises and falls. Bass inhabit the waters of the marsh, gyrfalcon have been seen hunting above it, and deer feed on the lush marsh grass of the many low islands. The bottoms of the tidal channels are densely covered with algae, sponges, snails, clams, crabs, worms, and a multitude of other forms of life that find food and security in these sheltered waters. One of the best known of all marshes, Nauset Marsh each year attracts thousands of visitors who take guided tours conducted by rangers of the National Park Service.

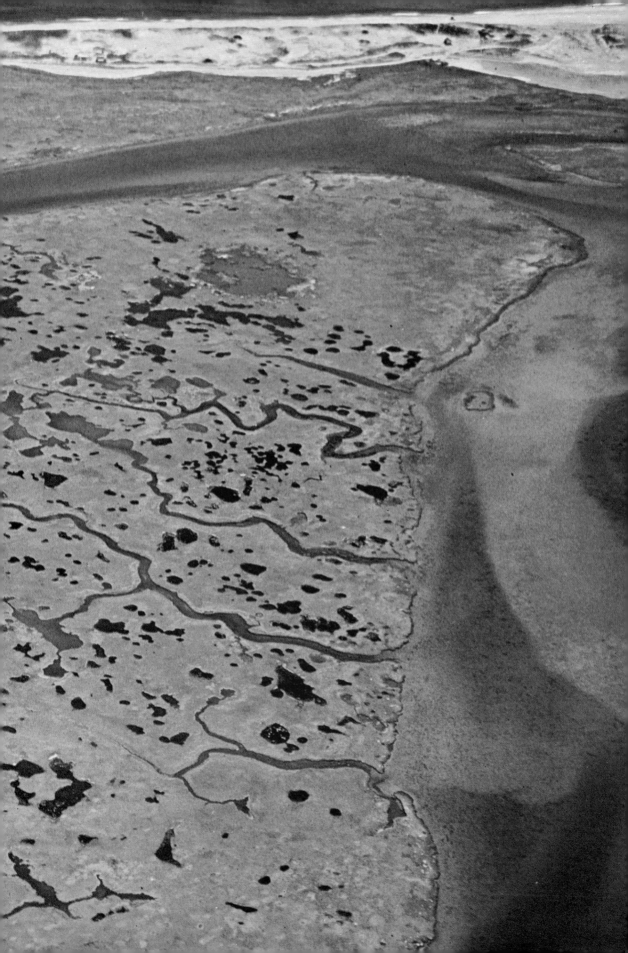

with tall grass. Because there is little or no slope to a tidal flat, wave action and runoff are slight, although it may drain fairly well at low tide. A marsh always holds water. The bottom consists of rich deposits of dark organic mud which originate in the decay of dead plants in the marsh and along the banks of tidal streams farther inland and is the source of an unpleasant smell at low tide.

Despite the drawbacks for humans, however, the tidal flat holds the greatest riches of all shorelines in the quantity of plants and animals living there. Even from its marshy edge, if you sit quietly, you can see more large animals than on other shorelines. In the East, you may be able to see the humps of muskrat lodges rising from the dense marsh grass. Occasionally you can see the muskrats themselves swimming along the ditches and streams of the marsh, or running through the grass. In the evening, bright-eyed, crafty-looking raccoons hunt along the shores.

Birds are everywhere, but you will need binoculars to span distances when you watch them. Some are close relatives of those from inland: seaside sparrows, sharp-tailed sparrows, red-winged blackbirds, and long-billed marsh wrens. Others are strictly shore types: clapper rails, willets, spotted sandpipers, and oyster catchers, to name only a few. These last shore birds, unlike many other creatures, live along both the Atlantic and Pacific coasts.

On a quiet day you may hear what sounds like wind sweeping through the marsh grass although the grass blades are still. If you investigate, you will find crowds of fiddler crabs (*Uca*) flitting across the mud to new feeding grounds. Among them, ignoring the bustle, will be an occasional

Although the vast expanse of a salt marsh may seem to be monotonous, definite patterns of zonation are noticeable from open water to elevated land. At the edge of a tidal channel in which thousands of killifish swarm, tall marsh grass fringes the bank. Beyond this, in the upper intertidal region, short marsh grass covers acres of rich mud. Quantities of organic detritus resulting from the decay of this grass and other grass are carried away by tidal currents. As the land rises slightly, marsh grass gives way to pickle weed and sedges, which are tolerant of salt mud but not of frequent tidal immersion. Animals of a salt marsh are mostly migratory or burrowing forms; the crabs, for example, retreat into their burrows when the tide rises and emerge to feed when it falls. In the tidal flat shown to the right, various molluscs, crustaceans, and worms burrow deep into the soft sediment, perhaps beneath an eelgrass bed. Certain mammals, birds, and reptiles find protected salt marshes highly suitable for nesting and feeding.

SALT MARSH

RED-WINGED BLACKBIRD

MARSH SNAILS

HIGH TIDE

SEDGE

PICKLE WEED

MUSKRAT

SHORT MARSH GRASS

PURPLE MARSH CRAB

FIDDLER CRAB

MUSKRAT

CLAPPER RAIL

WILLET

FIDDLER CRAB

purple marsh crab (*Sesarma*) feeding stolidly on short lengths of marsh grass. Eventually you will learn to recognize the different burrow entrances of each species. The purple marsh crab constructs a kind of hooded hut over the entrance to its burrow, which descends straight for a foot or so, then levels out into tunnels and rooms. The opening to a fiddler-crab burrow is either perfectly round or surrounded by a slight lip, depending upon the species.

Looking more closely into the vegetation bordering a tidal flat, and into any exposed mud, you will soon find a great many different kinds of animals. Marsh snails (*Melampus*) perch on the stalks of grass above the habitat of fiddler crabs. Worms of many different kinds, some of which are large and colorful, occupy the mud. Buried alongside the worms can be ark clams, tube-dwelling amphipod crustaceans, sea cucumbers, soft-shelled clams, and ghost shrimps (*Callianassa*). Crawling on the surface are transparent shrimps (*Palaemonetes*), sea hares, mud snails, and various mud crabs. Also on the surface, but immobile, are mussels, sea squirts, and oysters.

While the birds and some of the crabs are carnivorous, you can tell that the great bulk of the population eats decayed plant material, or detritus. Look at their many fine tentacles, filters, sieves, scoops, and other feeding devices. Nearly all tidal-flat creatures strain detritus from the water and mud.

Lugworms find mud flats so favorable that they reach populations as high as 82,000 to an acre. Since these creatures are over half a foot long and as big around as your thumb, it is obvious how rich in nutrients the environment must be to support them. Lugworms feed on organic matter

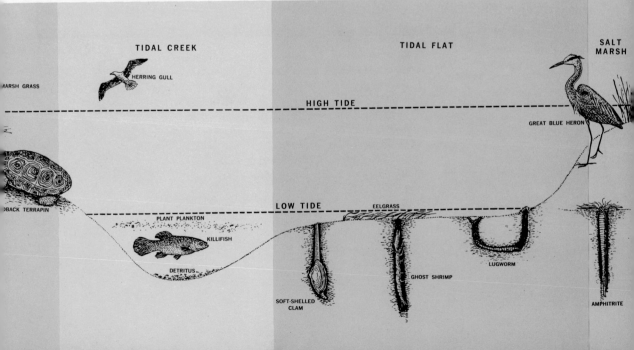

TIDAL CREEK   TIDAL FLAT   SALT MARSH

MARSH GRASS   HERRING GULL

HIGH TIDE

GREAT BLUE HERON

OBACK TERRAPIN

PLANT PLANKTON   LOW TIDE   EELGRASS

KILLIFISH

LUGWORM

DETRITUS

SOFT-SHELLED CLAM   GHOST SHRIMP

AMPHITRITE

MOUND BUILDERS OF THE COASTAL MARSHES

Found throughout most of North America, the muskrat is at home both in fresh-water ponds and streams and in the shallow waters of coastal salt marshes, especially along parts of the Atlantic and Gulf coasts. Mink, bald eagles, and many other animals prey on muskrats, but their greatest enemy is man; thousands of these dark-brown rodents are trapped every year for their sleek, dark fur. Even so, they remain abundant because each female can produce several litters of young each year. Watch for the V-shaped ripples trailing back from its chin as a muskrat swims across an area of open water.

Perfectly adapted to life in the water, the muskrat's oarlike feet enable it to swim at the rate of two or three miles per hour. The scaly eight-inch tail acts as a rudder, and the dense, waterproof fur increases buoyancy by trapping a layer of air. A muskrat can swim for fifty yards or more beneath the surface without coming up for air. Because its lips close behind the large gnawing teeth at the front of its jaws, the muskrat can nibble on plants even when underwater.

122

A group of muskrat houses (above) dots the placid water of a coastal salt marsh like miniature islands. As evening falls the muskrats emerge from their houses and spend the night foraging for food—mainly the stems and roots of marsh plants, but occasionally a few clams or other small animals as well. In many areas muskrats burrow into moist embankments instead of building mound-shaped houses. Built from the stems and leaves of dead marsh plants, roots, twigs, mud, and other debris, a muskrat house may be as much as four feet high and eight feet across. From an entrance beneath the water, a passageway leads to a snug, dry chamber above water level. Here the muskrat is relatively safe while it rests or cares for its young. As winter progresses and food grows scarce, the hungry muskrat may eat some of the dead plants in the foot-thick walls of its house.

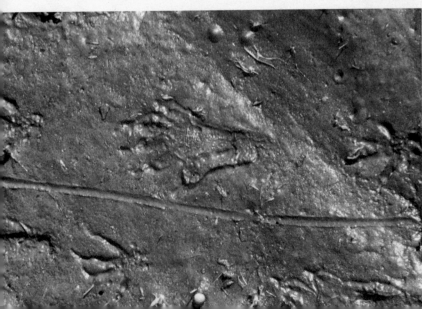

Telltale tracks across a mud flat reveal the route of a muskrat's nighttime wandering. Clumsy on land, the muskrat is a skillful swimmer. The large hind feet, each slightly webbed and fringed with short, bristlelike hairs, form efficient paddles. The rudderlike tail usually etches a distinct line in the mud between the muskrat's tracks.

A purple marsh crab squats before the entrance to its
burrow and nibbles on marsh grass, the staple in its diet.
Its burrow, which plunges down for a foot or so and then
branches into several side tunnels, is easy to recognize—
the entrance is sheltered by a mud hut.

in the mud, as do the mud snails which feed at the surface. Sometimes the great numbers of mud snails give marshy coves a particularly dark color.

All of the detritus (decaying organic matter) comes from the few kinds of plants that can grow in salt mud. These are mostly grasses and algae. One of the most common is marsh grass, *Spartina,* which comes in two forms—a variety that grows close to water in tidal creeks and a smaller species that covers large areas of flat marshland The remains of plants either sink to the bottom or remain suspended in the water, making it quite opaque.

The productive marshes

Ecologists, who study the relationships of living things to each other and to their environment, speak of "primary production." By this they mean the manufacture of plant material by photosynthesis. Rates of primary production in forests and wheatfields are extremely high, as you can see from the abundance of the plants. Yet marshlands exceed even these. In fact, primary production in salt marshes is greater than for any crop in the world except sugar cane. *Spartina* yields three times as much as the best wheat lands, without any cultivation by man. Marsh plants lock up the sun's energy in their tissues, or store it in sugars and starches. Later these substances, turned into detritus particles, supply food for marine organisms. Filter-feeding animals trap and devour some of the detritus, and bacteria break down much of the rest into dissolved chemicals that fertilize the mud flat and the ocean beyond. Both the rooted algae of clear waters and the vast blanket of photosynthetic plankton floating in offshore waters benefit. Plant plankton, of course, provide food for the majority of small or young animals of the ocean, which in turn nourish many fishes and even some kinds of whales.

Thus shoreline marshes, called wastelands by some, actually produce much of the nourishment for many forms of life

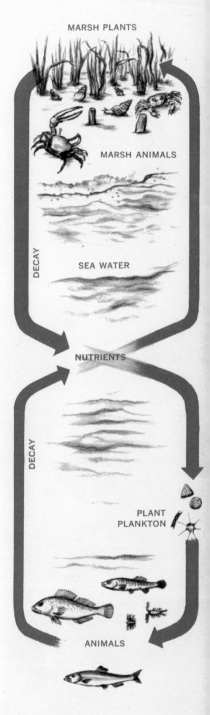

Coastal marshes nourish life in the sea. Besides providing food in the form of detritus (not shown here) for filter-feeding animals, the decay of marsh plants and animals releases chemical nutrients into coastal water, where they support the growth of plant plankton. Death and decay of plant plankton, and of those animals whose food chains are based on the plankton, once again returns the nutrients to sea water.

125

in the coastal seas. Destroying them by draining or filling to provide industrial sites can bring disaster to the animals and fish of the shore and the ocean.

Where one habitat meets another

The life of the salt marsh exists in zones. As on other shore areas, these zones are related to the rise and fall of tide; but they may be hard to trace because of the salts accumulating in the mud. At low tide, salt pools in a coastal marsh may, as a result of evaporation, contain water more than twice as salty as ocean water. This saltiness may severely limit the type of organisms present.

Tidal flats, which are closely linked to salt marshes, may exhibit much less evidence of zones. This is because of the lack of slope. If the flat sloped more, water would run off, carrying away much of the sediment. The existence of a muddy bottom shows how stable conditions are and, as a result, the same kinds of animals are found repeatedly over the entire expanse of a mud flat.

If you use a sieve to examine the bottom of a mud flat you may be disappointed. It will trap only larger animals you already know about, plus bits of plant material. Note how extremely fine the mud particles are. Obviously only those animals especially equipped to avoid suffocating in deep, dense clouds of fine silt can survive there. Lugworms have the equipment—indeed, they actually devour the mud to take out organic matter. Other kinds of tidal-flat animals have structures that keep the mud from clogging their gills and other organs.

A mud flat containing sand attracts a somewhat different population. Zoologists know that bottom-dwelling animals can sense differences in bottom sediments far slighter than our most sensitive instruments can detect. Each animal can find the size of bottom particles it likes best for a home and can also detect many other things, such as the organic content of the bottom. If you can determine a range of particle sizes as a mud flat gradually becomes a beach, you should be able to discover the particular zonation of each kind of burrowing animal. Some prefer mud, some sand, some different degrees of a mixture of both. The area in which mud and sand mix attracts the most animals. Mud provides many nutrients, while sand is better for burrows and tunnels.

From a crab's point of view, a stand of three-foot-tall marsh grass looks like a jungle. Decaying stems and leaves of dead grass in the rich organic mud provide nourishment for a vast community of animals.

Where one kind of habitat meets another and fuses with it, one finds an edge effect or, as ecologists call it, an *ecotone*. Other ecotones, for example, are the shoreline of a pond or the transition from field to forest.

Man-made shores

Geological changes, such as upheavals of continental rocks, are responsible for rocky shores. Other natural forces, events, and developments over thousands or millions of years produce other kinds of shorelines. Man too engages in activities that change the shore and even create entirely new shore situations.

Sometimes he builds a large stone breakwater in a region which for hundreds of miles has nothing but sandy beaches and tidal mud flats. Life quickly occupies it—the life of the rocky coast, not the beach and mud flat. Ages before man appeared, the larvae of fixed, or *sessile*, organisms floated past the beaches and flats with only an occasional opportunity to attach to a bit of driftwood. Then man came along, placed rocks and pilings in the sand, and within hours animal and

127

The arm of a stone breakwater across the mouth of a bay provides a rocky coast in an area of sandy shores. Man-made habitats of this sort are quickly colonized by plants and animals characteristic of rocky shores.

plant colonization would begin. In a matter of weeks, or at most months, the sessile forms had grown into an enormous, stabilized community. It is tempting to think that the animals and plants were waiting for such an opportunity, but this is not true. The world is populated as it is today because living things overproduce their young, which then scatter to every possible region on currents of wind and water or under their own power. If they find a niche to which they are adapted, they settle down and reproduce. If not, they die.

Some scientists have thought that certain forms of shore life could live in only one or a few places. Such experts have often been surprised. Living things turn up in parts of the world where they could not have been found a hundred years ago. Much of this extension of range results from man's activities in placing sea walls, breakwaters, jetties, buoys, and even wrecks in areas where there had been no solid surface to which sessile plants and animals could attach.

Elsewhere, along some rocky coasts, man has brought in sand for bathing beaches. Soon sand animals not usually found in the area populate the new artificial beaches.

It is not only currents that transport living things up and down a coast. The bottom of a ship provides a good place to live for many sessile animals that can withstand a strong flow of water. Along with certain algae, sessile animals attach themselves in great numbers to a hull. Then when a ship puts into a foreign port, larvae, eggs, or spores drop off and take up residence.

Many animals now distributed throughout the world no doubt spread in this fashion. For example, a small olive-and-orange-striped sea anemone (*Diadumene luciae*) found today along our East Coast originated in the Orient. Various worms, molluscs, hydroids, crustaceans, and rooted algae have traveled in this way. Today a book on the seashore life of our northern and mid-Atlantic coast must also cover the subject for the coasts of England!

Patterns of succession

What happens when man builds a solid structure in a sandy coastal area is a demonstration of the process of succession.

Perhaps you have left a boat in salt water and found, after some weeks, that its speed and maneuverability have decreased because of growths on the hull. A mariner calls this a fouled hull. When you examine the fouling growth you find that it is a definite community of plants and animals. With little effort you can watch the order—succession—of living things from the beginning as they colonize a new spot. The growth and the climax community are the same as on a rocky shore, or on new pilings or other man-made structures.

A boat is not necessary for your experiment. The easiest thing to do is to scrape bare a rock just below water level at low tide. You could do the same with a piling, if there are no rocks. Better still, suspend a board, a plate, or a piece of glass about a foot beneath a float. The float will rise and fall with the tide, keeping your test surface at a constant depth. Anchor or tie the float to a pier so it will not be carried away.

Inspecting the surface periodically, you will discover the order in which living things attach to it. The pioneers will be bacteria, followed shortly by protozoans and diatoms. To see these as individuals, you will need a microscope, but you can detect them because they form a slime that is easy to feel.

A few days later many more diatoms will be growing, coloring the surface a yellowish-brown, even giving it a furry appearance. There will also be small strands of green algae and the beginnings of a moss-animal (bryozoan) colony. The third stage may consist of larger bryozoan colonies, plus hydroids, some small tube-building worms, a few barnacles, and a few sea squirts. Next the animals of the third stage grow abundantly and are joined by a few mussels.

The final (climax) stage is a permanent association that remains together as a community unless the environment changes drastically. Climax stages vary somewhat with the kind of surface and exposure, so you should not always expect one specific community. Typical possibilities for the Middle Atlantic Coast are: (a) Mussels dominant, with annelid worms, tubeworms, and skeleton shrimps; (b) Barnacles dominant, with tubeworms and skeleton shrimps; (c) Tubeworms dominant, with sponges, bryozoans, and amphipods; (d) Tunicates dominant, but only if the other three dominant animals are lacking. You may find one climax community near another of a different sort. Exactly what factors determine which organisms live in a place is a matter of considerable scientific interest and is little understood.

Most boat owners, naturally enough, are not enchanted by

FOULING SUCCESSION

When the hull of a boat (or any other hard-surfaced object) is immersed in sea water, plants and animals begin to colonize it almost immediately. The sequence of fouling organisms shown here is typical for Middle Atlantic coastal waters. The first two levels are almost invariable, but what follows them may differ widely depending upon the kinds of swimming larvae that are present and upon environmental conditions.

Bacterial slime settles within the first hour.

Diatoms and protozoa follow within the first day.

Hydroids and bryozoa settle within the second to third day.

Barnacles and algae follow and cluster densely within a week, and a few mussels appear.

Finally mussels dominate, and only a few barnacles remain by the second month.

the fascinating biological world on the hull of a boat. Their main interest is in getting rid of the organisms.

The simplest means is the oldest—and requires the most work: scraping off the fouling organisms. This is an effective but only temporary cure. Ancient mariners did this, and so do a great many small-boat owners today. Another means was discovered accidentally long ago. Because fouling organisms belong to the ocean, they cannot survive in fresh water. Ships that enter rivers and dock at fresh-water ports are soon reasonably clean of foulers on their hulls.

The best method is to discourage the attachment of foulers in the first place. The ancient Phoenicians smeared arsenic and pitch on their wooden ships; the Romans tried lead sheathing. In the eighteenth century the British sheathed hulls in copper, which helped a great deal. Today some poisonous paints and plastic compounds keep foulers away for as long as eighteen months. You might experiment with various surfaces to determine which is the most and which is the least attractive to foulers. Some plastics remain remarkably free of fouling organisms.

Mangrove succession

Another quite different example of succession actually results in the construction of more shoreline. You have to visit the Everglades National Park in southern Florida, or particularly the Florida Keys, to see it.

In untouched regions in coves and on coral shores there are thick tangles of small mangrove trees. Look in the shallow water for very young trees. These are red mangroves— the pioneers—and they reach out into the shallow sea, taking root in coral sand and even penetrating coral rock. Once a few are established, more red mangroves grow in their shelter. By standing back and looking over the whole shoreline, you will note a distinct gradation of size—the smallest and youngest trees out the farthest, the largest slightly inland. Over a number of years, as mangroves take root in the shallow water, sediment is trapped around their many roots and stems and gradually builds up until exposed soil is formed. The actual shoreline is therefore advanced forward into the sea, and the island grows larger.

You will see that on the land behind the red mangroves there is another mangrove, the black mangrove, which suc-

By dropping a tangle of roots and prop stems into shallow water, mangroves gradually extend the shoreline as sediments and debris become trapped in the maze of stems.

130

ceeds the red after firm soil has been formed. The red mangroves keep advancing into the water; the black mangroves follow.

The fascinating plant-and-animal associations within a mangrove swamp in the Keys or on the Florida mainland deserve your thorough exploration. Florida mangroves do not grow nearly so large as those in Central and South America and in the southern Caribbean, but they form the same tangle of woody prop stems that hold up the trees and are so sturdy you can walk on them out over the water.

Locked for eons between layers of shale in Wyoming, these fossils are the remains of fish that swam in a sea which covered portions of North America nearly fifty million years ago.

Yesterday and today

As a mangrove succession shows, natural events can change the shoreline significantly within a few years. Over millions of years, changes in shorelines—and in mountains, rivers, and all other aspects of geology—are tremendous.

Because of this, you can come across marine fossils of animals that lived more than 60 million years ago as far inland as Montana and Iowa. In the southeastern part of what is now the United States, ocean waves from the same period, called the Upper Cretaceous, broke upon shores 300 miles west of the present shoreline. Everywhere there is evidence that the seas have invaded what is now land, and that they have receded at other times so far that the edge of the present continental shelf was the shoreline.

North America was discovered less than 500 years ago, yet the early crude charts drawn by the Spanish and British reveal that capes, bars, barrier beaches, river deltas, and other important features have changed significantly. In fact, if you visit a beach today and return in only a few years, you will be able to notice differences.

A great lighthouse, built far inland in 1825 on Cape Henlopen on the Atlantic coast, fell into the sea in 1926 as the shoreline retreated under and beyond it. In the same region, fishing trawlers hundreds of yards out to sea have brought up tree stumps still rooted in clay. In New Jersey and Delaware, beach erosion sometimes uncovers old marsh mud containing clear impressions of wagon tracks and hoofprints. The shoreline is never constant.

Thus the shoreline you see at any one time is only a temporary feature. Plants and animals follow as it migrates in-

EVERGLADES NATIONAL PARK

A young mangrove provides roosting space for cattle egrets and boat-tailed grackles. Eventually the wandlike seedlings that dot the shallows also will grow bases of prop roots. In the distance is a thicket of mature mangrove trees.

Searching for crustaceans, molluscs, and other morsels, a fragile-looking black-necked stilt wanders past a mangrove seedling on an Everglades tidal flat.

More than 2000 square miles of land and water at the southern tip of Florida make Everglades National Park a semitropical paradise. Alligators, manatees, zebra butterflies, tree snails—the abundance and variety of unusual animals is almost beyond belief. But the prime attraction is the incredible array of birdlife. Roseate spoonbills nest in the Everglades. Herons and egrets stand like sentinels in the shallow water of bays and tidal flats. Flocks of pelicans wing across the sky. Cormorants, anhingas, limpkins, wood storks, and many others live here.

Even the shoreline is varied. Great sandy beaches at Cape Sable are littered with exotic tropical shells. Jagged expanses of weirdly eroded limestone in other areas shelter chitons, sea urchins, and a host of other animals. But most characteristic of all are the dense mangrove forests that cover thousands of acres along the Park's coastline. Nearly impenetrable thickets interlaced by a maze of placid streams and rivers, they give way in the Gulf of Mexico and Florida Bay to a sprinkling of hundreds of low islands and mangrove keys. Here especially the wading birds congregate in spectacular nesting colonies. And here visitors come by the boatload to explore a fantastic subtropical wilderness that has been preserved for all people to enjoy.

Dignified and aloof, an American egret turns its back on the quarreling of a group of roseate spoonbills. Both of these birds nest in the junglelike tangles of mangroves that fringe the Everglades.

land or out to sea. While our own lives are too short to notice much change, you can see the temporary nature of the shoreline by studying a relief map that shows the topography of both the coastal plain and the continental shelf. You will have a hard time finding the exact line of the present shore —it could be anywhere!

The kind of shore at any particular location—rocky, sandy, or muddy, and having a gentle or steep slope—has much to do with at least the short-term changes. Often the slope determines whether mud or sand can be deposited. Shorelines that slope steeply produce violent wave action and a small intertidal area as well as little deposition of sand and mud. Those that slope gently have great expanses covered by tides, waves breaking far out, and much deposition. The steep slopes tend to be eaten away, the flatter areas to be silted up.

We have seen how living things, such as mangroves, can build new land. Mangroves, marsh grasses, and marine grasses of the tidal flats trap sediment, building shorelines and changing their nature. Coral also builds shorelines out into the sea: most of the state of Florida stands on an old coral reef. Heavy oyster populations leave shells that build up shallow flats. At low tide, there may be hundreds of acres of sharp-edged oysters out of water. Some kinds of worms also build up shorelines.

Yet despite all the variations and alterations of shorelines, you can easily become so well acquainted with the seashore that merely by looking at a shore you can tell what animals and plants live there, and by looking at organisms from the shore you can tell what kind of shoreline they occupied.

An abandoned anchor from the bark *Austria*, shipwrecked in 1887, lies among the pools on a Washington coast tidal flat. Encrusted by a mosaic of barnacles and draped with seaweeds, a discarded work of man finds new value as one of the many worlds of the seashore.

The Abundance
of Life

The world of the seashore provides a place to live for an astounding number of different organisms. Plants and animals themselves, by gathering together in complex communities, contribute a great deal to the creation of their own habitats. These communities are as important, and as interesting, as any other aspect of the seashore.

Perhaps it will be easier to understand the communities and how they work if you consider one such assemblage in some detail. The oyster is the world's most thoroughly studied marine animal. Generally speaking, studies of natural communities are fairly recent, but investigations of oyster communities were well under way in Germany in the 1870s. Hence an oyster bed (which is what the oyster community is called) can tell you a great deal about the rigors and successes of life along the shore.

It matters little which part of the North American coast you visit; oysters are everywhere. If you do not find the particular examples of animals in an oyster community that are described here, there will be others like them. Even if a community contains different species of animals, the same *types*,

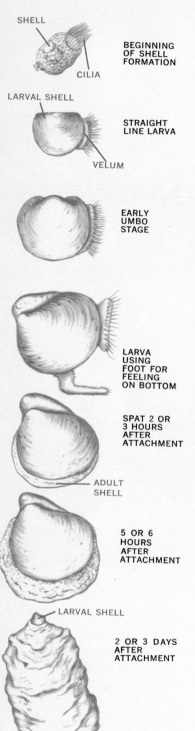

SEVERAL STAGES IN THE DEVELOPMENT OF AN OYSTER

SHELL

CILIA

BEGINNING OF SHELL FORMATION

LARVAL SHELL

STRAIGHT LINE LARVA

VELUM

EARLY UMBO STAGE

LARVA USING FOOT FOR FEELING ON BOTTOM

SPAT 2 OR 3 HOURS AFTER ATTACHMENT

ADULT SHELL

5 OR 6 HOURS AFTER ATTACHMENT

LARVAL SHELL

2 OR 3 DAYS AFTER ATTACHMENT

filling the same *ecological niches,* are found everywhere. An ecological niche is not a place but a way of life for a particular organism. Tides and shores exist all over the world and provide similar conditions. In an oyster community you will find filter feeders, parasites, predators, and so on, though the species differ from one place to another.

Oysters are sessile, bivalve (two-shell) molluscs that feed by filtering the water. They live together in enormous communities; most of these are below the surface in shallow bays, but you can sometimes find an oyster community exposed in a tidal flat during low tide. Oysters grow well in flats where the water changes regularly, removing sediment that could suffocate bottom-dwellers.

When conditions are right in bays and tidal rivers, oysters can form reefs as great as those created by corals in tropical regions. The oyster reefs outside bays along the coast of Louisiana cover a great many square miles. Half the entire world harvest of oysters is taken in Louisiana and in Chesapeake Bay.

Oysters are abundant because in one spawning an adult female can release over a hundred million eggs, most of which will be fertilized by sperm from nearby male oysters. This may occur two or three times a year for seven or eight years. If all the eggs of one female, and their descendants, were to survive, in five generations they would occupy as adults a space 250 times the volume of the earth. Fewer than 1 per cent of the young survive in temperate waters, in part because larger marine animals eat the microscopic larvae while they are a part of the plankton, in part because of the rigors of the environment.

After living less than two weeks as members of the plankton, the larvae metamorphose into tiny two-shelled molluscs and descend to the bottom, where they attach. Most of them, no doubt, descend to unsuitable bottoms and they die. But where there is a hard, clean surface, large numbers of little oysters do attach. Proper conditions may be hard to find on the natural bottom of tidal flats, but one kind of surface is just right: the shells of live or dead oysters.

Larval oysters may play an active part in choosing where they will settle. In laboratory tests they show a definite preference for shells rather than for glass, pebbles, bricks, and other hard surfaces—evidently they have an ability to select a site. The shells in the tests, incidentally, had no living animals in them, so the attraction of the little oysters most likely

Oysters, the most commercially valuable molluscs, are
gathered by hand at Drakes Estero on the California
coast. Elsewhere huge quantities of oysters are harvested
mechanically with dredges. To increase the yield of
commercial beds, oyster farmers often cover the bottom
with tons of oyster shells to provide places
for the larvae to become attached.

was a physical rather than a chemical matter. Live oysters, which certainly affect surrounding water chemically, would probably have an even greater influence.

At times you can find as many as a thousand tiny oysters, or *spat*, on one adult shell—packed on 670 to one square inch of shell surface. But 669 of these are candidates for extinction. Charles Darwin called similar situations "survival of the fittest," and while we know today that the matter is vastly more complex (chance has a large role), the one oyster to survive may well have had a quality that enabled it to overcome difficulties that killed the rest.

Animal associations begin inside the oysters. Some may harbor parasites that eventually destroy them—in recent years a microscopic parasite has killed millions of oysters along the Atlantic coast. Larger animals that reside within the oyster's shell usually do far less harm. One, the oyster wafer, is a small, apparently harmless flatworm, although it can injure weakened or sick oysters. Another, the oyster crab (*Pinnotheres*), feeds on plankton and organic matter brought in by the oyster's gills, but it may also nibble at the gill tissues.

The gills, incidentally, are remarkable organs that play an important role in the life of the community as well as of the oyster. They have numerous small beating hairs (cilia) that draw in water—up to thirty quarts an hour!—and then expel it from between the two valves of the shell. Not only do the gills serve as breathing organs by pumping the water in and out, they also collect food on their surface, carry food to the mouth, transport and excrete wastes, and secrete mucus. With the help of the gills, an oyster carefully strains planktonic food and detritus from the water, consumes some but rejects much of the nutritious matter. The rich, concentrated nutrients, including algae and microscopic animals, fall out of the shells and support multitudes of other filter feeders in the oyster community. Any fisherman can tell you that fishing is better over an oyster bed than over a more barren bottom. The fish come to feed on the many crabs, worms, and other animals that take advantage of the "wasteful" habits of the oyster.

Oysters cement themselves together in clusters, which oystermen call *hands*. Secretions of other animals in the community also help cement the hands. These strong, heavy clusters, with many crevices and holes, provide excellent hiding places and surfaces for a great variety of living things.

The oyster crab, *Pinnotheres ostreum*, is a member of a family of crabs that dwell either within the mantle cavity of various molluscs or in the tubes of burrowing worms. Although an oyster crab generally is considered a commensal with the oyster, it has been known to nibble on its host's mantle tissues, thereby becoming a parasite.

If you place a cluster in a tub or bucket of sea water and examine it carefully, you will find a number of different animals and plants. Many of the smaller animals will crawl out of their hiding places if you add a pinch or two of Epsom salt.

In every nook and crevice, for example, are tiny mud tubes. Inside live small horned worms, or spionids (*Polydora*). The horns are actually two long tentacles which the worm waves about energetically to collect suspended food. Horned worms especially like to attach along the lip of an oyster shell, where they filter the nutritious expelled water. Another species of worm, a free-moving nereid, wanders through the oyster community in search of rich feeding grounds.

Then there are the tubeworms (*Hydroides*), which build twisted masses of limy tubes oystermen call *coral*. Tubeworms compete for space with the oyster; they are joined in this contest for survival by a variety of other stationary animals. These include sponges, barnacles, sea-squirt tunicates (*Molgula*), bryozoans (*Alcyonidium* and *Membranipora*), many species of hydroids, slipper shells (*Crepidula*), jingle shells (*Anoma*), blue mussels (*Mytilus*), tube-building crustaceans (*Corophium*), and sea anemones (*Diadumene leucolena*).

Some of these small animals attract a strange fish, the naked goby (*Gobiosoma bosci*), which is a regular member of the community. It feeds upon the community's smallest members—worms and crustaceans. Tiny, almost completely without scales, it has a curious formation of fins on its undersurface. The fins make a suction disk with which it can hang onto hard surfaces when tidal or wave currents wash over it.

Plentiful food and surfaces for attachment attract many animals to the oyster community. Common residents include (*foreground*) an anemone, a cluster of slipper-shell snails, bryozoans, and a naked goby. In the background are sea squirts and several mussels.

Enemies of the oyster

Not all the inhabitants of an oyster community compete with or threaten the oyster simply by occupying scarce space. Many come to eat the oyster.

If the salt content of the water is as high as fifteen parts per thousand parts of water, sea stars and oyster drills can survive. A sea star is a serious predator of oysters. Fortunately, low salt and high temperatures of bays and estuaries or tidal rivers limit its numbers in summer, when oysters grow most actively. A sea star attaches its powerful tube feet to the shells of an oyster and slowly pulls to spread the

141

A group of inch-long
oyster drills *(right)* attacks
a bed of mussels. In a laboratory
experiment *(below)*, an
oyster drill begins to bore into
a mussel shell containing a
live oyster (part of the shell
has been cut away and covered
with a sheet of glass).
The bottom picture shows the
drilling mechanism. A secretion
from the accessory boring
organ on the right first weakens
a layer of the shell, then the
proboscis on the left is
inserted to rasp away the
weakened material.

shells. Then, when the shell opens, it turns its own stomach inside out through its mouth, wraps it around the oyster's body, and digests the oyster right in the shell!

Oyster drills (*Urosalpinx* and *Eupleura*) have been in business for 28 million years and are well equipped for attacking oysters. With chemical secretions and a rasping tongue (radula), an oyster drill slowly files a small, straight hole into the shell of the victim. The drill is the single greatest predator of young oysters (its diet also includes mussels and barnacles), and each drill accounts for an average of thirty-four oysters.

Another snail, the moon snail (*Polinices*), also bores into oysters, but creates a wide hole with a beveled edge, usually near the hinge of the oyster or clam it is attacking. A large conch or whelk (*Busycon*) preys upon the oyster in an entirely different fashion. It grabs an oyster with its muscular foot, then bangs the snout of its own shell against the edge of the oyster. Once the oyster shell is broken, the conch inserts the snout into the break and, by twisting, trims off enough of the edge of the oyster shell to thrust its feeding apparatus within.

You may find on the beach a shell pitted with dozens or hundreds of small holes. These are the work of the boring sponge (*Cliona*), which usually grows on oyster shells. The sponge bores into a shell to secure a footing. There is no mechanical drill, however, only a secretion that eats out little pits in the limy shell.

There are still more ways of attacking an oyster. In addition to animals living inside its shell, other creatures reside in oyster beds. Some of the largest are blue crabs (*Callinectes*), green crabs (*Carcinides*), and rock crabs (*Cancer*). Most numerous are several species of mud crabs. These small crustaceans, with their heavy, black-tipped claws, are everywhere in the community. Pick up a cluster of oysters and dozens of small, grayish shapes scuttle off to new hiding places. All these crabs, large and small, prey upon young oysters. A blue crab trims off the edge of the upper valve, opens it, and devours the soft body. Mud crabs, with their strong, knobby claws, can crack open small oysters and extract the meat.

Fish prey upon the oysters. Skates and rays eat young oysters. The black drum, an unusual fish with a powerful crushing structure in its throat, grinds up oysters and spits out the pieces of shell, swallowing only the meat. The toadfish, though, is actually beneficial to the oyster. Wrongly called oyster cracker, it apparently eats not the oyster but animals that either destroy or compete with oysters.

If the predators fed solely on oysters, the survival of the whole community would be endangered. Should the oysters be killed off, the community would be destroyed. A disaster that affected a relative of the oyster, the bay scallop (*Aquipecten*), illustrates this principle.

Scallops exist in large numbers only in beds of eelgrass (*Zostera*)—one of the few marine plants that produces seeds. In the early 1930s, a protozoan infection killed nearly all the

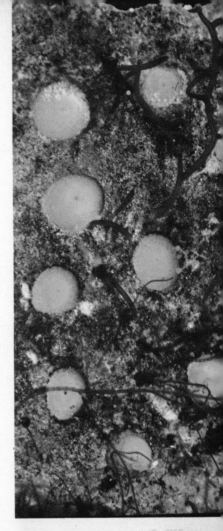

Tiny holes in an oyster shell were made by the boring sponge. The living sponge protrudes through the holes *(top photo)*, but most of its body lies hidden beneath the surface of the shell, as seen in the sectional view *(bottom photo)*.

143

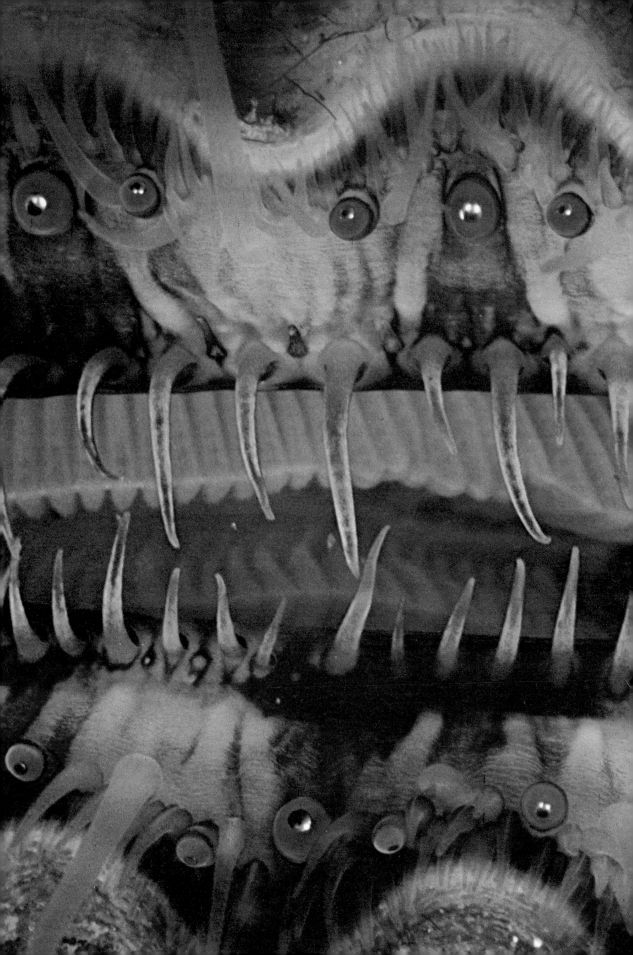

eelgrass along the Atlantic shore. Thereupon the flourishing bay scallop vanished from much of its former range. Dozens of species of plants and animals that had lived directly on the eelgrass also disappeared. As a consequence, the death of the eelgrass wiped out other organisms and destroyed the thriving scallop fisheries of Virginia and other coastal states. Although much of the eelgrass is back with all its associated life, the bay-scallop industry is still not back to its former level.

The oyster community

At this point it should be possible to summarize the roles played by various members of the oyster community. Any algae present are the *primary producers*, making sugars through photosynthesis and from them other plant materials. The oysters, their relatives the mussels, sea squirts, and all the other filter feeders extract microscopic algae and detritus from the water. They are thus the *primary consumers*, the animals that eat plants. Oyster drills, sea stars, and other predators feeding on oysters and mussels are *secondary consumers*. A crab or fish that devours a drill snail would be a *third-order consumer*, and so on. Nereid sandworms and many of the smaller crustaceans feed on waste material and much other organic matter in mud; they quickly clean out dead oysters. They are the *scavengers* of the community. The oyster crab can be thought of as a *commensal* which lives with the oyster without harming it or helping it, although when the crab eats an oyster's gills, it becomes a *parasite*.

A major reason for the size and complexity of the oyster community is its stability. The key members—the oysters— have long lives, and their generations overlap. Hence oysters do not appear and disappear from season to season or year to year. The stable oyster population provides a suitable habitat at all times for a wide variety of plants and animals.

Scallops swim by jet propulsion. When the two valves of the shell are snapped shut, the jet of escaping water moves the animal ahead.

Unlike any other bivalve, the scallop can see. Two rows of brilliant blue eyes, each complete with cornea, lens, and retina, enable the scallop to perceive approaching enemies such as sea stars. An escaping scallop occasionally darts off with such a burst of speed that it breaks the surface of the water.

THE HIDDEN WORLD OF
THE EELGRASS COMMUNITY

In shallow, fairly cool water along both coasts of the United States, great beds of eelgrass cover parts of the bottom. Thousands of ribbonlike leaves, each about a quarter-inch wide and as much as a yard long, form miniature forests in the shallow sea. Scallops swim by jet propulsion through the tangled maze of stems; crabs scuttle across the bottom. Eels, flounders, burrowing anemones, and many other creatures find food and shelter in this shadowed world of swaying blades. Even more remarkable is the community of plants and animals that inhabit the leaves themselves; the slender blades are often covered with dense growths of algae and hordes of small animals.

Only in recent years has the eelgrass community been studied in detail. In the early 1930s a parasitic infection practically eliminated eelgrass along the East Coast. As the eelgrass died, so did the flourishing Atlantic scallop fishery, for scallops are one of the most prominent members of the community. Fortunately the eelgrass recovered and once again inhabits much of its former range. Since the disaster, scientists have begun investigating the plants and animals that thrive wherever eelgrass grows.

One of the few marine plants that produce seeds, eelgrass also spreads by sending up new leaves from its branching underground stems. As a result, a single bed

One of the few seed-bearing plants that live in the sea, eelgrass produces eighth-inch-long seeds in small capsules along the blades. Nearly all plants that live in the ocean are seaweeds, or algae, and are far more primitive than eelgrass.

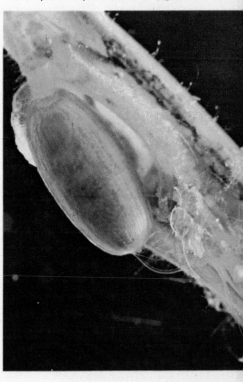

A hermit crab ventures from its dim retreat in the hidden world of the eelgrass community to feed in an open area. Scallops, flounders, eels, and many other creatures lurk on the sandy bottom of this underwater jungle, while overhead the ribbonlike blades are tufted with heavy growths of smaller plants and animals.

One of many molluscs that live among the eelgrass, a sea slug creeps slowly up a blade. Although the lower part of the leaf is completely free of fouling organisms, the upper part becomes densely cloaked with plants and animals.

The midsection of a blade of eelgrass
is dotted with limy tubes deposited
by coiled worms. The tiny worms
remain in their pinhead-sized tubes
and filter food particles from passing
currents. Plants along the edge of the
blade are red algae; the small
needlelike objects are diatoms.

The surface of an older blade of
eelgrass is thick with attached life.
At the center is a hydroid colony,
with its polyps extending their
tentacles. The surrounding tufts of
algae are coated by a layer of
detritus and diatoms.

may extend for many acres across the sandy bottom. Since
the plants take nutrients directly from the surrounding
water, they grow best in areas where waves and currents
produce a gentle stirring of the shallow water. As the
blades grow older and longer, they become increasingly
fouled with smaller plants and animals. Besides providing
a place for attachment, the eelgrass rises close to the
surface where light and oxygen are plentiful and currents
bring a constant supply of food particles and dissolved
nutrients.

Although the attached plants and animals may
completely cover the surface of the eelgrass, they are not
parasites. Except for possibly reducing the amount of
light that reaches its cells, they seem to have little effect
on the eelgrass. Interrelationships among the smaller
plants and animals, on the other hand, may be very
important. Recent studies have shown that algae on the
surface of a blade form efficient diatom traps; as many as
19,000 diatoms to the square inch may grow upon their
filaments. Detritus—particles of decaying organic matter—
also settles in thick deposits on the algae. The abundant
food supplies attract a great many grazing crustaceans,
molluscs, and worms. Some of the worms and crustaceans
also use detritus particles to build protective tubes, while

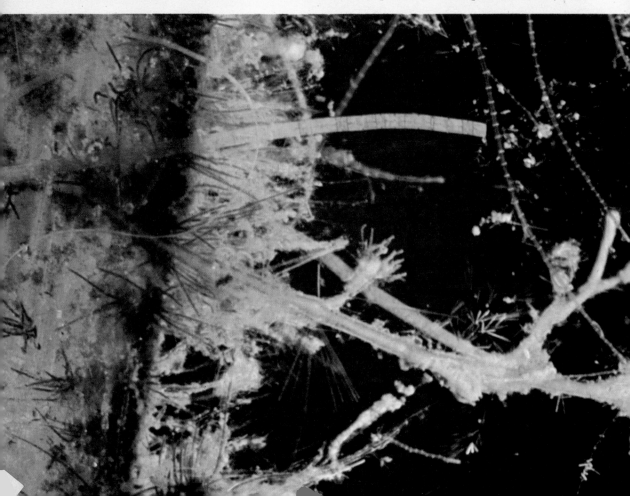

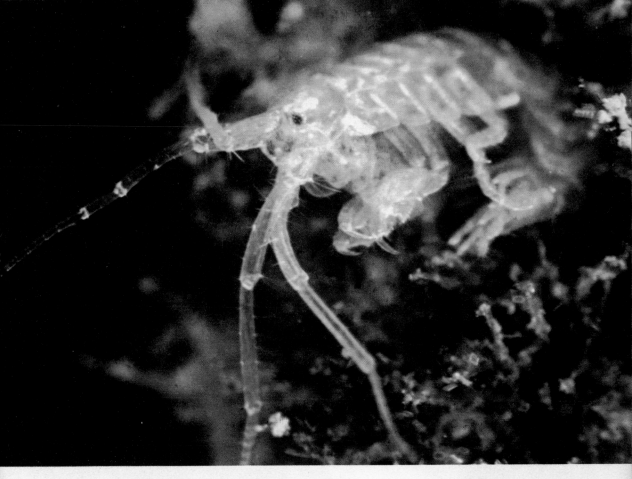

others deposit limy tubes of calcium extracted from the sea water. The tangled mat of plants on leaf surfaces also hides small animals from the view of predatory fishes.

The miniature plants in turn benefit from the activities of the animals. By feeding on detritus and diatoms, amphipods keep the algae's photosynthetic filaments exposed to light. This service is so important, in fact, that algae reach their maximum development about three quarters of the way up a blade of eelgrass; closer to the tip even very large numbers of amphipods cannot keep the surface clear of settling debris.

Scientists also have discovered that animal populations of an eelgrass community differ according to environmental conditions such as temperature, water depth, and current strength. In swift currents, for example, small tube-building species are the predominant amphipods. In quiet water, larger, more powerful forms become more abundant. In addition to varying with the seasons, populations of small plants and animals also seem to follow patterns of succession as they settle on the blades of eelgrass.

Scraping off diatoms with its clawed front feet, an amphipod feeds in a deep pasture of microplants near the tip of an old blade of eelgrass. The surface is so densely covered with algae, and they in turn with diatoms and detritus, that the blade itself is no longer visible.

Some changes do transpire with time. Certain members of the community disappear seasonally, or at least increase or decrease in number at certain seasons. Changes in membership of the community may even come about with tides and with day and night. In addition, individuals die, but are replaced as new generations of the same species arise. Some species may give way to others that do the same thing in the structure of the total community. Finally, even basic types of organisms may change, but this occurs only after a drastic change in the physical environment.

Living together

Surprisingly enough, many of the familiar shore plants and animals exist closely and in harmony with others. The burrow of the ghost shrimp, *Callianassa*, may contain not only a ghost shrimp but also a pea crab, a scaleworm, another smaller shrimp, or a certain kind of clam. *Callianassa* lives on both coasts and is easy to find, although a certain amount of digging is necessary. Similar situations exist in the U-shaped tubes of the parchment worm, *Chaetopterus*, where other species of crabs are present. The home of an echiurid worm, *Urechis*, may harbor crabs, gobies, clams, and scaleworms.

Adult horseshoe crabs generally have a number of small white flatworms, *Bdelloura*, creeping over the surface of their gills. These appear to have no effect on the crab. It in turn offers the worms nothing but a protected place to live, yet *Bdelloura* is found in no other place in the sea.

In a tide pool you may be startled by the sight of a sponge, a sea anemone, or a clump of algae crawling about. The algae seem to sprout long, pointed legs, but the legs belong to a spider crab, *Libinia*, that has fronds of seaweed attached securely to its back. The algae have a firm base to grow on, while the crab is well hidden from predators. A sponge that scuttles about is most unspongelike, but, if you carefully raise it a little, you will again find a crab is the source of the

Hiding beneath a hat of sponge held firmly in place by its two hind feet, the sponge crab goes unnoticed by most predators; since the sponge contains hundreds of tiny bonelike particles called spicules, few animals attempt to eat it. This little crab, common in the West Indies, is found as far north as the North Carolina coast.

The small white sea anemone *Diadumene leucolena*, a common resident of the oyster community, is shown here attached to a living oyster. The tentacles of this colorless two-inch sea anemone form a waving, poisonous net. The stinging cells discharge into small crustaceans and worms but cannot be felt by humans.

151

A cleaning shrimp hovers calmly within the ring of a sea anemone's stinging tentacles, apparently immune to their lethal venom. In addition to cleaning the anemone's surface of bits of organic debris, this colorful little shrimp may benefit its host by luring unwary fish within range of the tentacles.

action. This small, rounded crustacean, *Dromia,* breaks off a suitable piece of sponge, hollows it out and holds it over its back with its hind legs; *Dromia* is most reluctant to let go of the sponge disguise! Crabs also carry sea anemones, either on the back or in a claw, as a weapon against attackers. The stinging cells of a sea anemone provide effective defense for the crab.

In the warmer waters of southern Florida, certain sea anemones have small shrimps resting on their oral disks. The shrimps touch the poisonous tentacles of the anemone, yet seem to be immune to the deadly stinging cells. There are various species of these shrimps, some associated with corals, others with bottom-dwelling fish. They are known as *cleaning shrimps* and will even work on the vicious moray eel, removing parasites and diseased or dead tissue from the skin and bits of food from between the teeth. From sea anemones and corals they clean off silt and debris, and also, because they are bright-colored, they may lure hungry fish that are then caught by the anemone or polyp. There are also fish that clean other fish and get food in this way.

Some sea anemones are green, as are certain amphipod crustaceans and a number of other shoreline animals. The green color is not their own, but comes from chlorophyll in microscopic algae within the animal's body. Possibly there is an exchange of oxygen, carbon dioxide, and nutrients between the plant and the animal, but in many instances the animals, living among bright-green seaweeds, have a green color that may help them survive.

Some relationships, such as those of the eelgrass community described earlier, are more complex. Wherever hydroid colonies grow on rocks, pilings, or buoys, many small animals take up residence. One familiar hydroid, *Obelia*, grows into a miniature bushlike form. When you remove a tuft to a container and examine it under low magnification, you can see skeleton shrimps bobbing and bowing. An occasional isopod crustacean is present. Specialized copepod crustaceans, adapted to a primarily nonswimming life, dart and skip through the branching colony. A bizarre sea spider moves deliberately on eight long legs from one strand of the hydroid to another. Nearby, a sea slug or nudibranch browses on the hydroid polyps. The whole association is fairly loose, for most of the animals can live elsewhere, but they do especially well in this particular grouping.

Vacant tubes of the feather-duster worm are often occupied by a small amphipod shrimp. Another tenant, a colony of bryozoans, forms the pitted crust on the surface of the tubes.

A large amphipod *(lower left)* and several caprellid shrimp find food and shelter among the tangled branches of a hydroid colony.

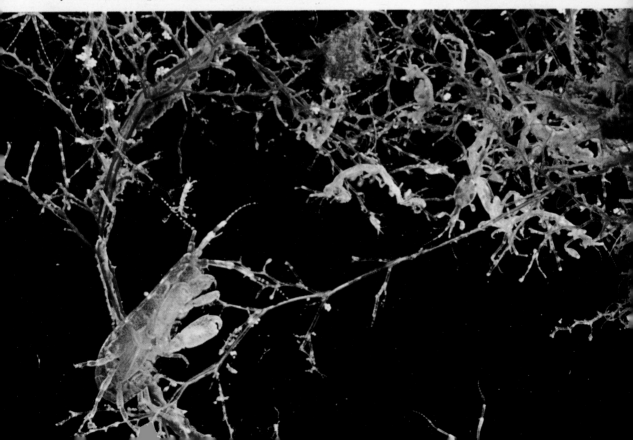

The empty shell of a moon snail
provides a home for a
hermit crab and living space
for a mossy colony of the
hydroid *Hydractinia.*

Scallops and oyster drills can become heavily fouled with organisms that benefit from being attached to a mobile base —algae of various types, tubeworms, bryozoans, hydroids. At times the host animal is so covered it is hard to identify. This could be an advantage, for although the host cannot move so easily, it is also not easily found by predators.

Another well-known association is composed of a hermit crab and a hydroid colony, *Hydractinia,* which grows on the snail shell occupied by the crab. *Hydractinia* is found nowhere else in the sea. If you collect several dozen hermit crabs along the East Coast, a few of the shells should have a soft, pinkish, fuzzy coating. Under a magnifier it will be seen that the covering consists of several types of polyps, all members of the same colony. Each type has a specific function—feeding, defense, protection against mechanical injury, and reproduction. The result is a division of labor among individuals of the same species, each kind of specialized polyp depending upon the others for some vital function.

Hermit crabs do not support *Hydractinia* alone. Turn one over and look at the aperture of the snail shell used by the crab. Crowded into the cavity may well be two species of slipper shells, horned spionid worms, young mussels, and scaleworms. If slipper shells attach to the outside of the hermit crab's shell before *Hydractinia* can grow, the hydroid colony will not appear.

On the West Coast, similar hermit crabs often become covered with dense clusters of barnacles. Along the California coast, boring sponges may grow on a moon-snail shell occupied by a hermit crab. Secretions from the sponge soon dissolve the shell and the crab finds itself in a living home— the sponge.

Loggerhead sponges in shallow water off the Florida Keys provide homes for a multitude of smaller animals. Slender fish, algae, worms, and crustaceans inhabit the labyrinth of chambers and canals of these large sponges. In one such sponge, more than 16,000 snapping shrimp and other small crustaceans were found.

These are but a few of the associations along the shore. Maybe you can add to this list dozens of similar relationships. No one knows how many there are altogether. New associations of marine animals are being reported constantly as the seas and their shores are explored further.

154

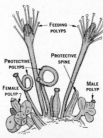

Magnification reveals the horde of specialized individuals in a *Hydractinia* colony. Long-tentacled feeding polyps capture food to nourish the entire colony. The heavy armament of stinging cells on protective polyps defends the colony against predators and helps paralyze prey. The attached medusa buds on reproductive polyps shed eggs and sperm into the water to produce the individuals that bud into new colonies.

Specialists everywhere

A number of major adaptations that improve the chances of survival along the shore are:

1. *Structural,* as in the barnacle, a crustacean that is adapted to the sessile way of life.

2. *Physiological,* having to do with the functioning of an organism.

    a. *Behavioral,* as shown by the mole crab, which migrates up and down a beach with the tide.

    b. *Biochemical,* as demonstrated by the oyster, which can stand a wide range of salinity in the water.

    c. *Reproductive,* as seen in the vast numbers of mussels that "set" on bare rocks after swimming as planktonic larvae.

These are, even so, only a few of the special adaptations you will find. Consider the molluscs.

Limpets and chitons, common inhabitants of the rocky intertidal zones, have home spots to which they return when the tide goes out. As time goes on, these spots grow increasingly visible, for the shells of the living animals wear away a deeper mark on the rock face. In the case of chitons, scars or depressions on the rock become deeper as they are occupied generation after generation. It is estimated that some chiton homes are at least a thousand years old! A chiton leaves its home spot at night to browse on nearby algae, and returns during the day to remain tightly sealed, especially when the tide falls.

During low tide periwinkles, one of the most common intertidal snails, seal themselves to the rocks with mucus which then dries. On windy days, the seals may break and the periwinkles fall into the water below with little splashes.

The abalone, a large edible snail from California, hugs rocks under the water with such tenacity that it can withstand a pull of more than 400 pounds. To remove one, you must pry it up quickly with a knife before it can clamp down with all its muscular strength.

Some sea slugs have acquired a remarkable ability to set up a defense system by making use of another animal's weapons. These slugs lack shells and would seem to be easy tidbits for predators, but few are eaten because they have an unpleasant taste. A species that lives among hydroid colonies has an additional defense, however. Hydroid polyps have stinging cells consisting of capsules, each containing a hollow, poison-filled thread with a sharp point. Normally

An armament of secondhand stinging cells and an unpleasant flavor protect the shell-less sea slug from predators.

they are exploded on contact. Yet in some way the nudibranch can eat such polyps without causing the stinging cells to go off. Inside the sea slug, the loaded capsules from the hydroid migrate until they lodge in the skin, pointing outward. There they once again act as protective devices, but this time for the animals that ate the organism these devices were supposed to protect! The nudibranch continues to eat hydroids, thus replenishing its armament.

Another adaptation or specialization is seen in the sea hare, a large snail-like relative of the nudibranch. It lives in warm water along both coasts, where it swims gracefully by, rippling wide, winglike fins that run the length of its body. When it is disturbed, it ejects a cloud of purple fluid that is poisonous and repulsive to attackers.

The bivalve molluscs also have their specialists. Some boring clams, highly modified from the general clam type, enter clay, wood, and even rock by twisting and cutting as smooth a hole as can be made by any man-made device. The ultimate in the boring clams is the shipworm, *Teredo*. Not a worm at all, this is a specialized bivalve with a body far too long for its tiny shell. Valves of the shell have evolved into sharp cutting edges with which the worm bores into wood. These creatures do vast damage to wood submerged in the sea—piers collapse, boat hulls leak—nothing wooden is safe unless it has been treated with chemicals. If you discover a piece of driftwood shot through with small holes and tunnels, the chances are it is the work of shipworms. These creatures, incidentally, somehow avoid breaking into each other's tunnels even in a piece of wood crowded with them. There is another borer, an isopod crustacean (*Limnoria*), which also tunnels into wood, but makes larger holes that may join.

A powerful sucking foot enables the chiton to cling firmly to rocks; movable overlapping plates allow it to bend its shell to fit the contours of the surface.

Echinoderm specialties

Spiny-skinned animals (*echinoderms*) include sea urchins, sea stars, sea cucumbers, sand dollars, and brittle stars. They are quite unlike any other group. For example, sea stars and sea urchins propel themselves across the bottom with feet moved by hydraulic pressure rather than large powerful muscles. Their special water-vascular system, an arrangement of canals, valves, little muscular bulbs, and tube feet with suction disks, allows them to walk on any surface. It enables a large sea star attached to a smooth rock to with-

157

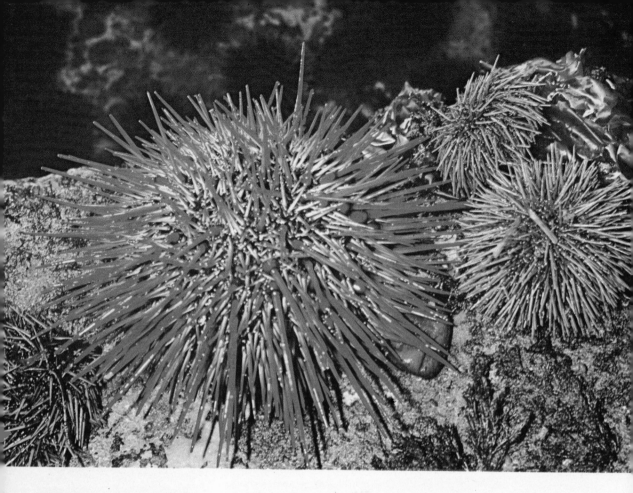

Since each spine is attached by a ball-and-socket joint, a sea urchin's bristling armament is movable. Probe at its body with a stick and all the nearby spines will turn and point menacingly toward the source of irritation. When it loses a few spines, an urchin simply grows replacements to fill in the gap.

stand a pull of more than a hundred pounds. With this great suction a sea star can open a bivalve mollusc.

The mouth parts of a sea urchin make up one of the most remarkable structural devices in the world. These animals are radially symmetrical—essentially circular, like a dome, without a head or left and right sides. Body structures emerge from the center of the animal like spokes of a wheel. Because two jaws are not possible, sea urchins have five jaws joined together to form an intricate but highly effective scraping mechanism. The jaw structure is so unusual that the ancient Greek philosopher and naturalist Aristotle noted its resemblance to a lantern. To this day, biologists call it *Aristotle's lantern.*

At the approach of a sea star, scallops jump off the bottom and swim away by jet propulsion. The cause for their alarm has been discovered only recently. The upper surface of the arms of certain sea stars gives off a secretion known as *ecto-crine* to which some animals are particularly sensitive.

Hermit crabs also become agitated when a sea star is in their midst. The presence of the star can cause a keyhole limpet to extrude its mantle (shell-secreting tissue) from under the edge of the shell and also through the opening at the top of the shell. The mantle continues to flow out until the whole shell is covered by living tissue, a condition never otherwise seen. Perhaps a sea star's tube feet cannot hold onto a soft, living surface as they can to a shell.

Probably the most remarkable response to ectocrines occurs when certain anemones are confronted with a species of sea star from the Pacific Northwest. If the star touches the anemone, the normally sessile animal breaks free of the bottom and swims off by convulsively jerking its body. If it is touched repeatedly with a sea star's arm, it finally loses the ability to react and sinks into a state of shock for a time. Even a fluid extract from the sea star makes the anemone flee. Such anemones actually have special nerve centers for this kind of response.

Only a few ectocrine reactions are known at present, but biologists suspect that they are important to a wide variety of marine animals. For example, barnacle larvae settle more heavily on surfaces coated with extracts made from adult barnacles than they do on unprepared surfaces.

The swimming larvae of the mud snail, *Nassarius*, settle in great numbers in the sediments of tidal flats. If these same sediments are heated artificially to high temperatures to de-

Reacting to an approaching sea star, a sea anemone quickly retracts into a tight mound.

Unlike other sea stars, whose larvae swim freely in the plankton, the blood star hunches up to form a brood-pouch, where it shelters its eggs until they transform into miniature adults.

Although its clattering call is a familiar sound in
salt marshes, the secretive clapper rail is seldom seen.
At the least alarm, the long-legged, henlike rail slips away
through the marsh grass. Its nest, frequently covered
by an arching canopy of grass, is usually built on higher
ground in the marsh. Even so, storm tides sometimes destroy
the nest and scatter the eggs or kill the downy black chicks.

stroy all organic matter, the larvae no longer settle. Again, certain marine flatworms produce fewer young when the adult population is high than when it is fairly low. Something about the crowding of adult worms prevents excessive reproduction. On the other hand, brittle stars crowd together in huge numbers in some spots but are completely absent in other seemingly identical areas. Do ectocrines given off by individual brittle stars cause more to seek them out? The explanation for all these occurrences and others may lie in the production of chemicals that bring about responses in other individuals. If you discover peculiar activities or reactions by shoreline animals, particularly involving sea stars, note the fact carefully and send your questions or findings to a marine laboratory. It may be a well-known phenomenon; it also may not be!

Shoreline specializations are not restricted to the smaller marine animals. All shore birds are adapted to feeding and breeding on rocky or sandy coasts or mud flats. For example, the purple sandpiper, which breeds in the Arctic and winters on the Atlantic coast, feeds almost exclusively at northeastern rocky shores and at man-made breakwaters. It goes only as far south as there are convenient breakwaters at close intervals; today this is not much farther than New Jersey. Two species of the rail, a common marsh bird, occur in regions of specific salinity: the king rail lives most often in marshes that have about four parts of salt per thousand parts of water, while the clapper rail usually resides in marshes of more than seven parts salt per thousand of water. Biologists would like to know if the salinity affects them directly or if a difference in diet separates the two species.

Specialization and reproduction

Special adaptations in a whole species do not arise overnight. Through the earth's history, changes in living things come about and are passed on through two processes acting together: mutation and natural selection.

Mutations are sudden changes in the inherited makeup of an organism caused by such things as heat, chemicals, and ultraviolet and other forms of radiation. Almost all such changes are harmful, so that living things having a mutation are likely to die out. Occasionally, however, a mutation helps a plant or animal to survive, making it in one way or another more efficient than others of its species. Here is where natu-

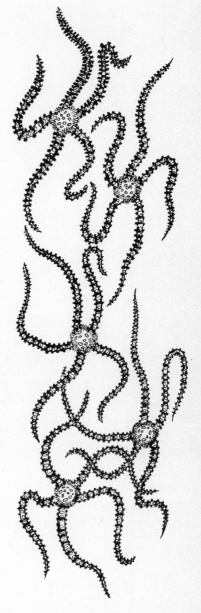

Although brittle stars sometimes gather by the hundred on the ocean floor, how or why they are attracted to each other is not precisely known.

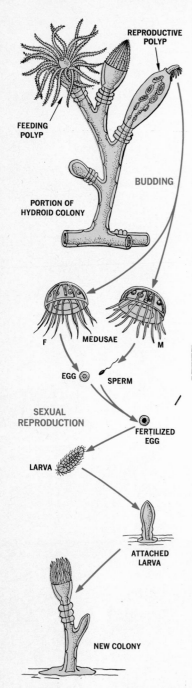

REPRODUCTIVE
POLYP

FEEDING
POLYP

BUDDING

PORTION OF
HYDROID COLONY

F   MEDUSAE   M

EGG   SPERM

SEXUAL
REPRODUCTION

FERTILIZED
EGG

LARVA

ATTACHED
LARVA

NEW COLONY

ALTERNATION
OF GENERATIONS
The attached hydroid generation produces new polyps and medusae by
budding. The free-swimming jellyfish
(or medusoid) generation reproduces
sexually to form the larvae that develop into new colonies.

ral selection comes in, for the individuals best able to survive
tend to live longer and have more surviving offspring. Gradually their kind becomes more numerous. Increasingly their
new and more successful trait is handed down from generation to generation. The physical environment changes, too,
so forms of life that were once successful in a particular
environment may not continue to be successful. The seashore
has always been a kind of proving ground: through the ages
it has been both an active, changing frontier of the sea and
the last outpost of the land.

It is through the process of reproduction, then, that species of plants and animals are able both to survive and to
change through time. Reproduction results in a multiplication of numbers, and the means by which organisms increase
are almost endless. There are, however, only two basic kinds
of reproduction: the familiar pattern in which males and
females produce cells that join to create a new generation
with characteristics from both parents, and the simpler, far
older method of simply breaking apart. The second type of
reproduction is known as *budding*; in this process each
separated part grows into a new individual. Budding offers
the advantages of speed and great numbers in reproduction,
but sexual reproduction gives succeeding generations many
more chances to change in form or function through the
mixing of hereditary traits and the passing around of beneficial mutations.

A tide pool is a good place to look for budding in animals,
and even to perform a few experiments. Sea anemones often
reproduce simply by dividing in two, from the base to the
crown of tentacles. Some species multiply more rapidly, however, by pinching off a whole ring of small buds from the
flat, muscular base. Each fragment then grows into a miniature of the original anemone and gradually increases to full
size.

Hydroids, relatives of sea anemones, possess an elaborate
kind of budding in which some individuals differ from
others. Certain individuals budded off are not polyps, but
tiny jellyfish that swim away. In this fashion the hydroid,
normally a sessile colony, is distributed over a wide area. The
offspring of the jellyfish, which reproduces sexually, later
settle to the bottom and grow into a new hydroid colony.
This is called *alternation of generations*, for one generation
reproduces sexually, the next by budding. The hydroid then
has the advantages of each kind of reproduction.

162

Sponges bud wholesale and may carpet entire pools, rocks, or pilings. So simple are they that breaking them up, cutting them to pieces, or even straining them through sieves does not kill them. Whatever remains merely continues to grow and bud off more sponge.

Fortunate accidents

Suppose you find a ribbon worm or a brittle star and pick it up, only to have it come apart in your hand. Does it die as a result?

Ribbon worms live under stones in the lower intertidal zone and beyond. Certain species, the large white *Cerebratulus* for example, break into many fragments with the slightest handling. *Cerebratulus* is quite a worm (up to seventy-five feet long), and when it falls to pieces there is a lot of worm scattered around. This does not kill the worm, however, for each fragment gradually grows into a new worm, a process known as *regeneration*. In experiments with *Cerebratulus,* it has been possible to grow new worms from pieces only one five-thousandth of the original worm!

The ability of brittle stars to fragment their bodies gives them their name. They lose their arms easily when picked up or irritated. They can lose *all* their arms plus the upper half of the central disk of their bodies. The severed arms die, but the disk will grow another upper half and new arms.

Their relatives, sea stars, also have some ability to regenerate lost arms, but not to the degree of the brittle star. If

The medusa stage of *Gonionemus* is shown here. In this species, the hydroid generation is minute and short-lived. In other species the hydroid generation may be conspicuous and the medusa stage reduced.

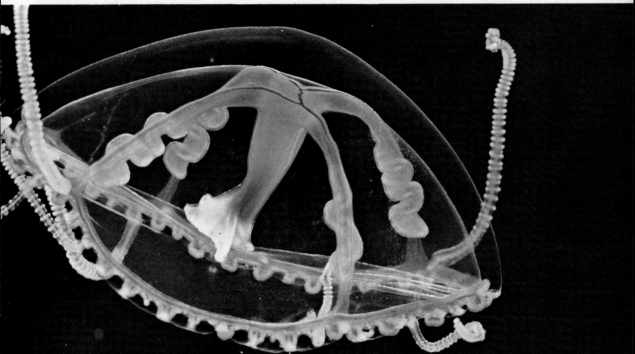

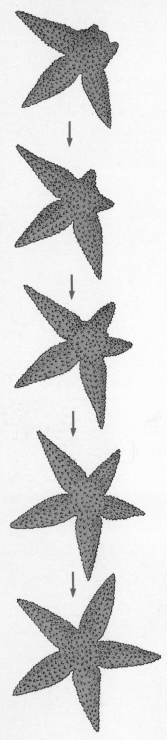

an arm breaks off with a bit of the central disk attached, however, the arm will grow a new body and, in turn, new arms. Years ago oystermen used to chop up sea stars in an attempt to kill them. All this did was to increase the number.

Some of the strangest examples of losing parts of the body are found in sea cucumbers, which, like the stars, are echinoderms. When attacked by predators, certain species throw out some of their internal organs through a rupture in the body wall. Others cast off their entire feeding apparatus. If the attacker eats these peace offerings and does not further disturb the sea cucumber, it will live to regrow new organs.

Lobsters and crabs are able to lose a few legs or claws without danger to them, but only a certain number of appendages can be discarded. If too many were lost, a crustacean would not be able to move about or feed. By careful observation you can find the precise place at which a crab's leg will be cast off: a kind of presealed wall through the base of a leg that prevents bleeding to death if the appendage has to be discarded. The loss of a leg stimulates a crab or lobster to molt sooner than it normally would, for it is only through successive molts that it can regenerate the limb. While regeneration is going on, the animal craves calcareous foods—the lime in the shells goes to strengthen its outer covering and the formation of the new limb.

Although regeneration is not reproduction, it does allow animals to survive to reproduce. Nevertheless, the excessive fragmentation and regeneration found in ribbon worms and sea stars might almost be thought of as a kind of reproduction that turns a bad thing (injury) into a good thing (more individuals).

Two of a kind

Sexual reproduction requires the manufacture of sperm cells by a male and egg cells by a female, but among many marine animals it is hard to tell which is male and which female. For example, about half of all marine snails have both

Streams of sperm flow from a sea urchin's reproductive pores. As soon as one individual begins to spawn, others nearby are immediately stimulated into shedding millions of eggs and sperms into the water. Fertilized eggs develop into free-swimming, transparent larvae that transform after several weeks into small, bottom-dwelling copies of the adults.

164

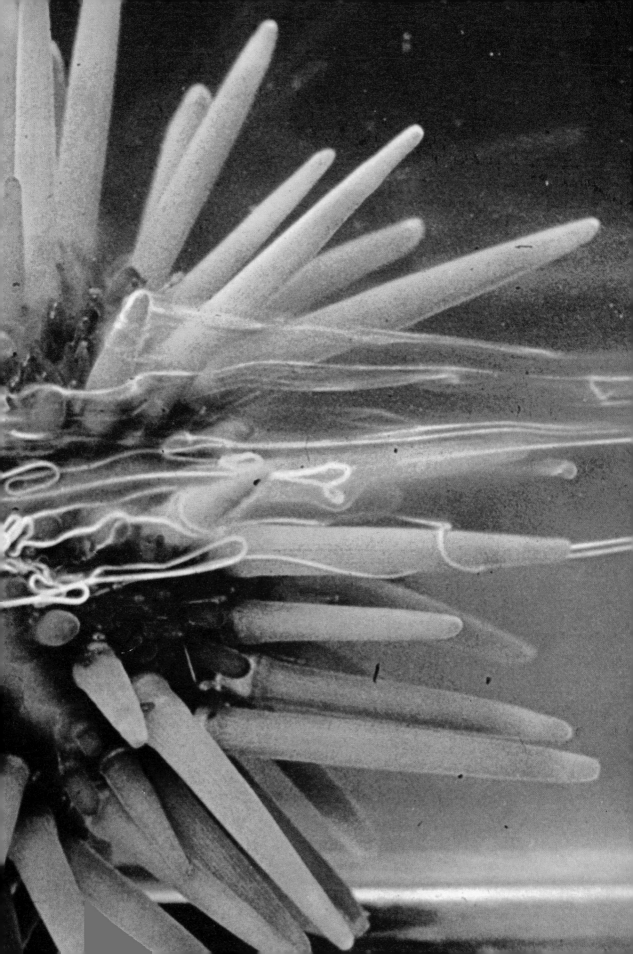

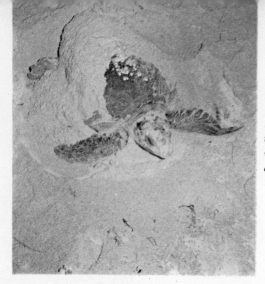

A huge loggerhead turtle—her shell is nearly a yard long—emerges from the sea on a summer night to lay her eggs. Resting in a shallow basin in the sand, the turtle has scooped out a nest hole with her hind flippers and is about to deposit her eggs.

SEAFARING LOGGERHEADS COME ASHORE TO LAY THEIR EGGS

Atlantic loggerheads, gigantic turtles that sometimes weigh 300 pounds or more, spend most of their lives at sea. But on summer nights, especially in June, they return briefly to the land to perform the compelling task of laying eggs. At scattered sites along the southeastern and Gulf coasts of the United States, the females lumber up from the surf and explore the sandy beaches for suitable nesting spots. Using her hind flippers, each turtle scoops out a nest eighteen to twenty-four inches deep—as far as she can conveniently reach with her flippers—then settles over the hole to deposit her eggs. One or two at a time, the moist leathery eggs drop like golf balls until a hundred or more fill the nest. The turtle then replaces sand over the nest, tamps it down with her flippers, and finally camouflages the site with a layer of loose sand. Her labors completed, the exhausted turtle plods back to sea, never again to pay the slightest attention to her eggs or young.

Once the turtle has begun the urgent business of depositing eggs, almost nothing can distract her. Lights, voices, the movement of onlookers— she remains oblivious to all.

Leathery golf-ball-sized eggs drop into the
eighteen- to twenty-four-inch-deep nest
in the sand. When laying is completed,
the turtle will pack sand over the nest
and then camouflage the site with loose
sand before lumbering back to sea. Even
so, marauding crabs, raccoons, and egg-
hunting humans often discover the nests
and steal the eggs.

About two months later, a parade
of hatchlings emerges from the
sand, usually all on the same
night, and the two-inch-long
turtles set off on a bold journey
to the sea.

sexes in one individual. Some of these are both male and female at the same time; others are males in early adult life, then turn into females later.

As with the oyster, the rate of egg production among most shore animals is staggering. Sea slugs can produce 800,000 eggs in a lifetime. Sea hares are capable of laying 41,000 eggs in a minute, and a female produces a total of nearly half a billion in the seventeen-week laying period. For very large sea hares the figures could be three times greater.

When crabs carry soft masses of fertilized eggs under their abdomens they are known as "sponge" crabs. Lobsters doing the same thing are said to be "in berry." A female lobster can carry as many as 97,000 developing embryos on the append-ages of her abdomen. Although they are protected while attached to her, the survival rate of young lobsters drops severely once they become larvae and swim off in the plank-ton. If two out of every 10,000 lobsters live long enough to reproduce, the species will not die out. Certainly the sur-vival rates of most young marine shoreline animals are low indeed. Nevertheless, there are so many larvae circulating through the coastal sea in currents and waves that almost every available habitat will surely be found and occupied.

Some studies of reproductive cycles have surprised biolo-gists. More than a century ago, an English army surgeon who was also an amateur naturalist found that barnacles were not molluscs, as had been believed. He watched the production of larvae by adult barnacles; when he examined the young he saw that they were obviously crustaceans. After a period of development they swam to an unoccupied sur-face, turned over, attached, and began to grow the limy shells of adult barnacles.

A number of vertebrate animals reproduce in the shoreline environment. Marine turtles, for instance, must come into beaches where they excavate nests and deposit their eggs. You might think this happens only on tropical islands in the Caribbean or South Pacific, but at least two species of turtles lay eggs on our Atlantic coast. The great loggerhead turtle buries her eggs, a hundred or more, on open beaches in the

Thousands of eggs, each about a sixteenth of an inch in diameter, adhere to the underside of a female lobster "in berry." A walking incubator, she carries the eggs for nearly a year before they hatch.

Gulf and along the Carolina, Georgia, and Florida coasts from April to August. Peaks of egg-laying usually come in June. The smaller diamondback terrapin, an inhabitant of tidal creeks and estuaries, constructs nests on beaches and in salt marshes of the Atlantic states as far north as Cape Cod during May and June. It seldom lays more than a dozen eggs. When you consider these events, it is apparent that the activity of marine turtles is just the reverse of that of the ghost crab. Both cross the water–land barrier to deposit eggs, but turtles come in to land and ghost crabs go out to the water. The sea turtles are land animals that have gone to live in the sea, and ghost crabs are marine animals that have invaded the land.

Most coastal birds and mammals also reproduce at the shoreline. Terns, skimmers, and gulls nest among the dunes and on grassy shores; auklets, murres, and puffins lay their eggs on ledges or in crevices of steep rocky coasts in the north. Along the West Coast, the California sea lion comes ashore in June when each female gives birth to a single pup. The large bulls take up stations on the beach; and not long after the pups are born, the adults breed. The pups learn to swim in shallow water before going to sea with their mothers.

No matter what the means of reproduction, therefore, or the place in which it occurs, the multiplication of numbers

The purple sea snail attaches its egg capsules to the underside of the frothy, cellophanelike float that keeps the fragile adult drifting with the currents at the surface of the sea. Several small goose barnacles are hitching a ride on this snail's shell.

of shore animals allows them to populate widely separated habitats. But by far the great majority of all larvae and young animals are soon eaten or destroyed in the waves and on the shores. As a result, almost every kind of shore plant and animal has developed the capacity for creating vast numbers of spores, eggs, or larvae that overcome the dangers of water movement, distant travel, and predation.

The great migration

When you walk along a shore, you take a tour back into history for more than a billion years. What plants and animals you find there are not simply oddities, or even relics of times past, but highly successful forms of life that evolved into their present ways of existence hundreds of millions of years ago. Through becoming adapted to their individual niches or ways of life, they have been able to live successfully for countless generations with little change in form or habit.

Once all life was restricted to the sea. Today even man remains linked to it; our body fluids maintain a constant salinity, and proportions of other ingredients in the blood also resemble those of the ocean. Echoes of the rhythms of the sea are found in the reproductive cycles of many land animals, including humans. The shore animals of today exhibit even more obvious evidence of how life has developed from most ancient times.

The water-vascular system of the echinoderms, the sea stars and their relatives, contains little other than sea water brought in through a sievelike filter on the upper surface of the animal. Here the sea itself is put to work inside an animal's body through a complex system of tubes and valves. Circulatory systems in other kinds of animals may have had similar origins.

Many animals of the intertidal shore have means of reducing water loss when they are exposed. The limpet and chiton clamp down, the barnacle and mussel close their shells, amphipod crustaceans seek cover under wet seaweed, and

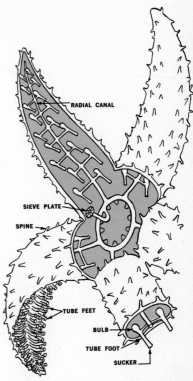

A sea star can walk six inches a minute on its hydraulic tube feet. When the bulb at the top of a foot is contracted, water is forced into the tube to extend the foot. By gripping a surface with the sucker at its tip and then contracting the foot, the sea star simultaneously pulls itself forward and forces water back into the bulb in preparation for the next "step."

A colony of male sea lions basks in the sun just beyond reach of the surf at Point Reyes National Seashore, California. More robust males, who defeated these bachelors in mating battles, are gathered in breeding rookeries on offshore rocks, where each boasts a harem of as many as twenty females.

171

burrowing beach forms descend to wet cool regions beneath the sand. Others have developed watertight coverings, making possible a gradual invasion of the land.

Certain crustaceans have come out of the sea to take advantage of greater opportunities for feeding on beaches and higher rocks, but they must return to the sea or to wet sand to breed and to moisten their gills. Only a few have gone far enough in this kind of adaptation to be free of their oceanic past. Once again, even we are not entirely free of the need for moisture. The membranes of our lungs, like those of all land animals, must be constantly moist. The embryos of reptiles, birds, and our own mammalian group develop in a watery medium.

Although they may exhibit adaptations for life on land, modern shore animals, of course, are not our ancestors, nor are they even similar to those creatures of the past from which we are descended. The fact remains that land-invading forms of life exist today in great numbers, just as they did in the distant past. The migration from sea to land continues. But we owe our existence to other creatures that long ago left the sea, entered fresh water, and then invaded the land.

The line of descent from the beginnings of life is a long one. The shoreline and shallow seas were the scene of the

Although modern vertebrate animals are all related, the line of descent is not direct. By 500 million years ago all invertebrate groups were in existence, evolving toward modern forms. One line of invertebrates, however, developed into primitive fishlike animals. Their descendants evolved along several lines, one of which developed into modern fish, and another into primitive amphibians. These early amphibians, in turn, produced the lines that led to modern amphibians and to primitive reptiles. The reptiles later gave rise to both birds and mammals.

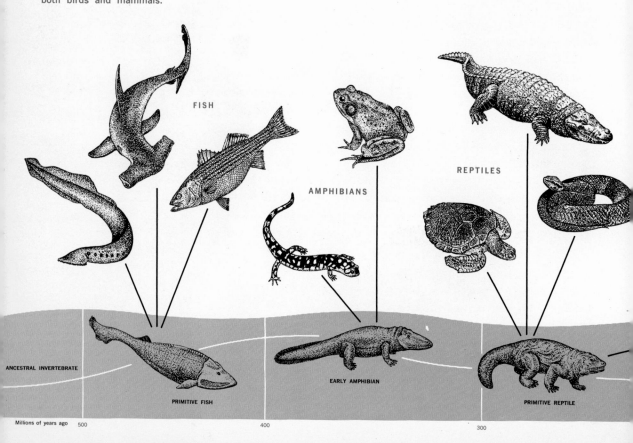

FISH

AMPHIBIANS

REPTILES

ANCESTRAL INVERTEBRATE

PRIMITIVE FISH

EARLY AMPHIBIAN

PRIMITIVE REPTILE

Millions of years ago   500   400   300

birth of the first living things. Here, in the past as today, the temperatures were favorable, light illuminated the water, and wave and current action concentrated organic matter in a narrow zone. While we are not sure whether the first organized matter preceding life occurred in shallow coastal waters, which is generally believed, or in the stormy atmosphere of the ancient world, we suspect that the substances consisted of amino acids and, later, proteins—which are made from amino acids. These compounds were assembled by the energy from ultraviolet light or lightning discharges. After millions of years they developed the ability first to make more of their own kind from raw materials in the sea, and then to organize the materials into increasingly complex patterns. Gradually these events caused primitive life to develop in shallow water, more than two billion years ago. Perhaps the life of that time was similar to blue-green algae of today, or perhaps it was more like bacteria, or even single-cell animals. Records of all these are found in fossil deposits. Such fossils, however, are exceedingly rare. So much has happened to the earth since they were first laid down that most of them have been destroyed.

Life eventually radiated from the seacoast into streams and tidal flats, and on up into fresh water. It was only much later that organisms invaded the deep sea.

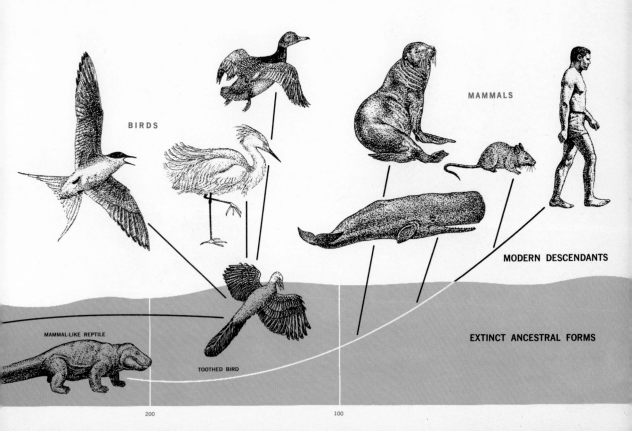

MAMMALS

BIRDS

MODERN DESCENDANTS

MAMMAL-LIKE REPTILE

TOOTHED BIRD

EXTINCT ANCESTRAL FORMS

200

100

At a very early time, more than 500 million years ago, all the major groups of animals without backbones were already established in shallow seas clustered along shores, where most of them have remained ever since. Green plants, originally marine algae, invaded the land about 500 million years ago, becoming fairly watertight as they did so. These plants set the stage for the invasion of land by plant-eating animals 140 million years later. The first true animal migrant from the sea seems to have been a kind of scorpion not unlike modern desert scorpions.

Today along a shore we can find simple members of our own animal group—the *chordates*. A chordate has a nerve cord running close to its back surface and a stiffening of the body just beneath the cord. Chordates also have gill slits on the sides of the head. These features recall fish. Fish, frogs, reptiles, birds, and mammals are all chordates, but highly developed ones. The simpler examples at the seashore include sea squirts, tongue worms, and lancelets. These distant "cousins" are more closely related to us than is the most highly developed insect, crustacean, squid, or other invertebrate (animal without a backbone). The primitive chordates of today tell us, as fossils never could, much about our distant origins in ancient, shallow seas.

Estuaries (tidal rivers) were probably highways for the migration of fish from the sea to inland fresh water, from which the first vertebrates emerged on land. Although invertebrates such as the scorpion came ashore from the sea, we know that our ancestors emerged from fresh water. Many pieces of evidence tell us this, including both fossil remains and our own kidneys, which are similar to those of fresh-water fish.

Some biologists believe that modern estuaries continue to serve as a route to the invasion of land. Blue crabs, shad, and many other fish and other invertebrates that live in tidal rivers, or invade them periodically, may be the ancestors of fresh-water animals and even land animals of the future. In the world today there are fish that emerge from water to crawl about on land and crabs that climb trees.

The glare of sunlight illuminates a placid inlet and, in the distance, the broad expanse of Chesapeake Bay on the Atlantic coast. Estuaries such as this, where fresh water mingles with that of the sea, probably were the avenues through which animals long ago migrated from the sea to fresh water and, eventually, to land.

The Flow of Life Energy

Animals obtain building materials and energy by eating other organisms. Living things use the materials of life over and over again—no new substances come to our world from beyond. These materials have been in constant circulation for over two billion years, and will continue to be used by all life to come. But the energy that makes it possible to put the same substances together time and again to form new living organisms does come from outside. It has to, for—unlike the materials of life—energy used by a plant or animal is eventually lost in the form of heat or motion, never to enter life processes again. The only continuing source of new energy is the sun.

The sun not only supplies the energy for all life, at the seashore and everywhere else, but holds the earth in an elliptical orbit that produces the seasons and tides affecting all life at the seashore. Seasonal temperature extremes influence animal migrations and life cycles, and erode the shore by ice expansion and searing heat. The sun's heat puts into motion the ceaseless winds that drive distant waves toward the land and maintains the water cycle so important to life. The waves crash upon beach and rock, moving sand, boulders, and living things about.

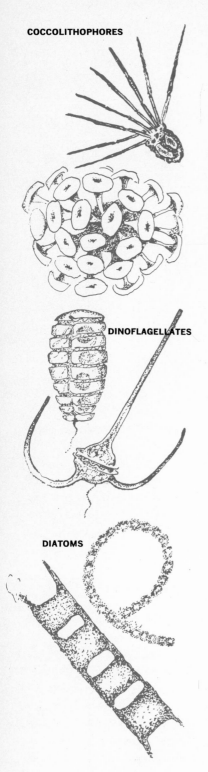

COCCOLITHOPHORES

DINOFLAGELLATES

DIATOMS

The average distance of the sun from the earth is 93 million miles, yet the light emitted by our star travels to us in a little over eight minutes. Some of its radiations are harmful, but the atmosphere and the dust particles suspended in it absorb most of these. Ultraviolet, for instance, is so filtered that little of its destructive effect remains when it reaches sea level. Water absorbs light so rapidly that marine plants are limited to shallow, clear coastal waters, particularly in the intertidal region and just below. Here every minute on a sunny day 4000 horsepower of energy fall on every acre. The areas of greatest primary production in the world are regions associated with or near the coast—if not the actual shoreline, then plant plankton offshore, salt marshes, mangrove swamps, or rich alluvial plains not far inland.

Microscopic producers

The primary production of microscopic marine algae, photosynthetic members of the plankton, nourishes many bottom-dwelling filter feeders and most of the free-swimming plankton feeders. Once eaten by first-order consumers, the algal energy and materials are on their way through a long chain of animals.

Microscopic floating plants of the ocean, known as *phytoplankton*, are mostly diatoms, with lesser numbers of small motile forms, the dinoflagellates. Because of their abundance, much smaller kinds of plants, the *coccolithophores* or yellow algae, may be as important in nourishing marine animals as the yellow-brown diatoms, but not enough is known about their distribution or their productivity to enable us to be certain.

Diatom production reaches staggering levels during the brief blooming periods when currents in the water stir up nutrients they need. Diatoms can divide into two new cells every twenty-four hours and may be 60,000 times as numerous in spring as in winter. Diatom populations as high as 72 million to a cubic foot of water have been reported. Under such conditions the animal plankton, which depends upon these plants, also increases. The numbers of plankton grazers —certain fish (herring, whale sharks), baleen whales, crustaceans, oysters, mussels, and others—are usually good indicators of the degree of productivity of an area. The principal swimming grazers are tiny copepod crustaceans, which

may number up to 3000 to a square foot of surface water. There can be as many as 100 billion copepods in a square mile offshore and in the water that washes over rocks and beaches. A single copepod can have in its stomach at one time more than 120,000 diatoms, which suggests the great efficiency of copepods as harvesters. A small fish feeding just off a beach might be able to collect 50,000 copepods in short order, and then, in turn, be eaten by a larger predator. No wonder filter feeders and predators find food so plentiful along the shore!

Mussels are good examples of sessile animals that filter out plankton organisms. An adult mussel can remove 100,000 planktonic larvae in a day's time. There may be 3.5 million mussels to an acre of salt marsh and an even greater density in smaller areas. A biologist counted 9200 very young mussels to a square foot in a particularly heavy set on an old barge wreck. Theoretically, a square yard of mussels might remove up to 100 million larvae in twenty-four hours. With

The copepod shown here, one of the most abundant members of the coastal plankton, carries a mass of eggs in the pouch attached to its tail. Within a week of hatching, the larvae are mature and able to reproduce again.

179

Mussels growing shell to shell
on the lower intertidal rocks
form an efficient living filter.
Just one adult can strain
as many as 100,000 planktonic
larvae from the water in a
single day.

so many larvae being eaten, it is small wonder that plants
and animals in coastal waters produce young in quantities
beyond our imagination.

For example, one apparently insignificant crustacean, the
sand shrimp *Crangon*, is enormously abundant wherever it
lives, and in addition a single female may be carrying up to
8000 eggs. Most of these become free-swimming larvae, but
their fate after that is hard to predict. Obviously enough
survive to continue the species.

At times, especially in the spring, there can be some 3000
different kinds of larvae in a quart of sea water. This figure
is not the number of individual larvae in the quart, just the
different species!

Soon after a bloom of plant plankton (phytoplankton) has
reached its peak, the populations of the minute plants begin
to diminish as a result of (1) grazing by the animals, (2)
the decrease in available nutrients, and (3) lessened light.
Why should light in coastal waters grow dim as summer
approaches? The blanket of surface plankton itself effectively

180

reduces the amount of light filtering down through the water.

Animal plankton decreases further in late summer and early fall, because of a decreased food supply and also because of the fact that many planktonic larvae have developed into larger nonplanktonic forms. After another fall bloom by algae, the populations of floating, drifting life drop during the winter to the lowest point in the year.

The great blankets of diatoms floating over the coastal seas of the world are unequaled in their total production, yet the larger algae of shorelines should not be overlooked. Weight for weight, a seaweed can produce as much organic material as a diatom, but because it can grow only in certain areas, the total mass of seaweeds is slight compared with the vast tonnage of microscopic floating plants.

Larger seaweeds are not so important in the food chain as are diatoms for another reason. A seaweed may be quite a big plant, and it is composed of organic matter concentrated in a firm structure both while it is alive and for a while after it dies. Dead seaweeds break loose from their attachments and often are cast up on a beach where intertidal and land scavengers can eat them. But if they are not washed ashore, they sink rapidly. Usually they are quickly covered with sediment and may not be eaten by marine scavengers at all. Thus the nourishment contained within seaweeds is often lost to other forms of marine life.

Planktonic diatoms, on the other hand, are so small they float easily, supported by the density of the water and their own flotation devices, including spines and oil droplets. After death they sink extremely slowly, decaying and disintegrating on the way down and releasing nutrients into the water. The organic matter of a diatom is gone by the time its tiny shell finally comes to rest on the bottom. It is no wonder that diatoms, and other less numerous planktonic plants, are considered the first and most important harvest of the sea.

Spines on their silica shells help keep diatoms afloat near the sunlit surface of the sea.

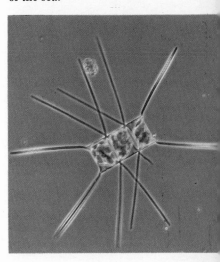

The role of animals

If you like clams and live near a shore, you have probably tried digging them from sand flats. You have to work hard to get even a rather small number, and perhaps you are not impressed with the size of the clam population. If you could

Magnified to 1500 times
its actual size, a diatom's
jewel-like beauty is revealed.
Thousands of species of these
single-cell yellow-green algae,
all basically similar in structure,
exist in nature. Their intricately
sculptured silica shells are
formed of two valves that
fit together like a lid on a box
(not visible in this
photomicrograph). Yet the form
and sculpturing of the shell
of every single species is
different, and a diatom may
resemble anything from a
pillbox to a cigar.

Diatoms are so minute that
millions may exist in a gallon
of sea water. During a
plankton bloom there may be
so many floating near the
surface that they actually
discolor the water. Because
of their abundance, diatoms
sometimes are called the "grass"
of the sea. By converting the
energy of the sun into the basic
food of nearly all marine
animals, they form the
indispensible first link in almost
every food chain in the sea.

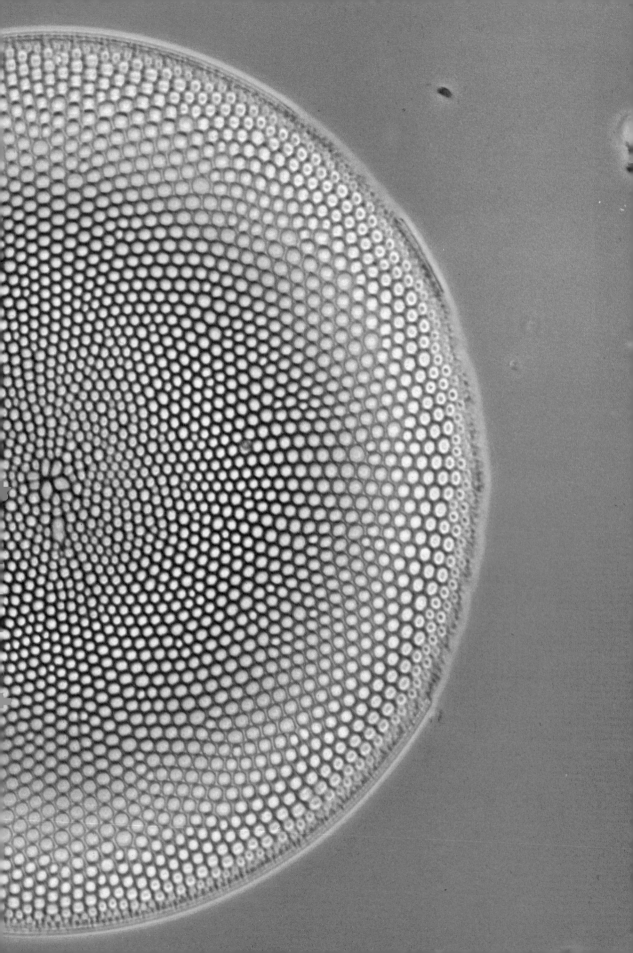

inspect fishery records, however, you might change your mind. In Delaware, a typical area of only a few thousand acres across yields 12.5 million clams each year to amateur and commercial clamdiggers. Removing these clams seems to have no permanent effect, for the same area keeps producing enough to allow this rate of harvesting year after year.

In the same locality 8 million blue crabs are caught each year, again with little apparent harm to the crab population. This does not mean, of course, that we could remove an increasing number each year. A time would come when the basic breeding population would be so reduced that there would not be enough larvae to occupy the available living space after being preyed upon by carnivorous marine animals.

The food web

Suppose you keep a careful record of the activities of a sand shrimp or some similar form living just below the water line, and of a ghost crab found above the high-tide mark. What do they eat? What eats them? What are their travels and migrations? As you accumulated information you would begin to put together a part of a food-web pattern of the shore.

Do not be misled by size of an organism as an indication of where it stands in a food web. To be sure, most second-

Violent surf during a 1939 hurricane dislodged these hardshell clams from the offshore sand and heaped them on a Long Island beach. Despite the wholesale destruction, clam populations soon recovered as larvae again colonized the area.

and third-order consumers (carnivores) are larger than their victims, but there are exceptions. An oyster-drill snail, for example, may attack a bivalve mollusc many times its own size. The size of primary consumers (animals that eat plants) is not particularly influenced by the size of their plant food, although planktonic vegetarians have to be larger than the diatoms they eat.

When a consumer animal eats a plant there is a transfer of energy, but the loss is very high. For example, from all the sunlight that shines on a diatom as it floats at the surface, the diatom traps in its own substance only three tenths of 1 per cent of the total energy received. Animal plankton eating the diatoms retain about one one-hundredth of 1 per cent of the original sun energy, and fish eating the animal plankton end up with less than three one-thousandths of 1 per cent of the solar energy!

Another way of looking at this is to view yourself as the ultimate consumer. If you should gain a pound from eating a bluefish, for example, you would be consuming the equivalent of production from 10,000 pounds of diatoms! The activities of living, or metabolism, are primarily a one-way flow of energy, and most of the energy is continually being lost as it is transferred from one level to the next.

Roughly, the decrease in energy received and retained can be thought of as a pyramid. Ecologists recognize two versions. In a *production pyramid* the amount of organic matter (and therefore of energy) is progressively less the further along a food chain it is found. The *pyramid of numbers*

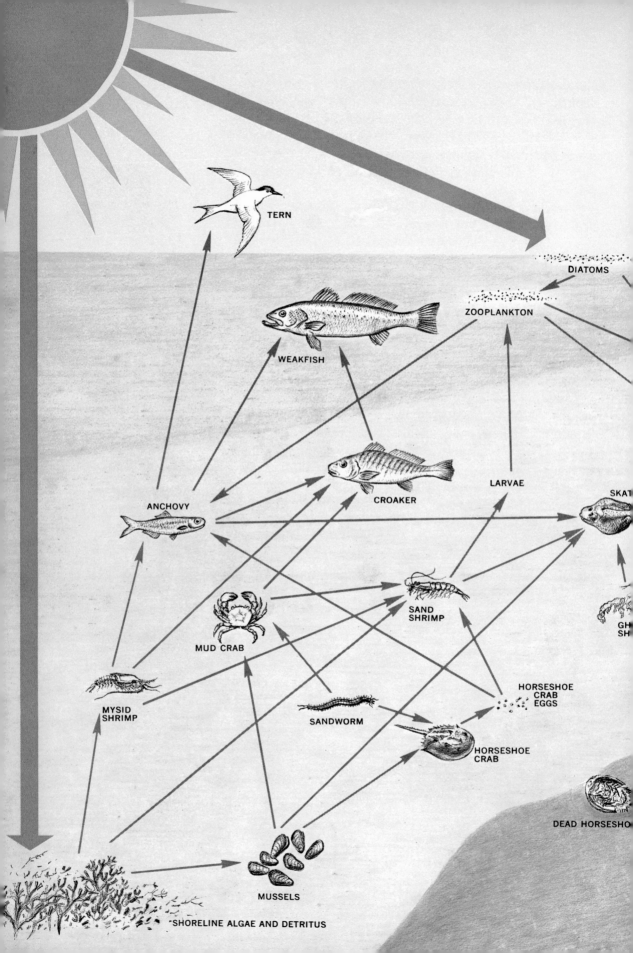

TERN

DIATOMS

ZOOPLANKTON

WEAKFISH

CROAKER

LARVAE

SKAT

ANCHOVY

SAND
SHRIMP

GH
SH

MUD CRAB

HORSESHOE
CRAB
EGGS

MYSID
SHRIMP

SANDWORM

HORSESHOE
CRAB

DEAD HORSESHO

MUSSELS

SHORELINE ALGAE AND DETRITUS

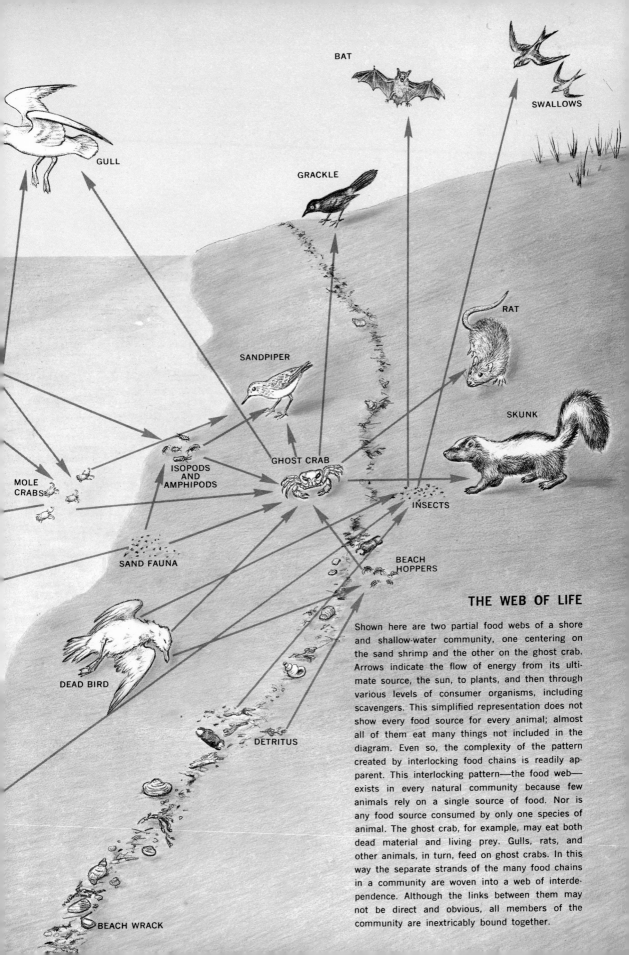

BAT

SWALLOWS

GULL

GRACKLE

RAT

SANDPIPER

SKUNK

ISOPODS
AND
AMPHIPODS

GHOST CRAB

MOLE
CRABS

INSECTS

SAND FAUNA

BEACH
HOPPERS

DEAD BIRD

THE WEB OF LIFE

Shown here are two partial food webs of a shore
and shallow-water community, one centering on
the sand shrimp and the other on the ghost crab.
Arrows indicate the flow of energy from its ultimate source, the sun, to plants, and then through
various levels of consumer organisms, including
scavengers. This simplified representation does not
show every food source for every animal; almost
all of them eat many things not included in the
diagram. Even so, the complexity of the pattern
created by interlocking food chains is readily apparent. This interlocking pattern—the food web—
exists in every natural community because few
animals rely on a single source of food. Nor is
any food source consumed by only one species of
animal. The ghost crab, for example, may eat both
dead material and living prey. Gulls, rats, and
other animals, in turn, feed on ghost crabs. In this
way the separate strands of the many food chains
in a community are woven into a web of interde-
pendence. Although the links between them may
not be direct and obvious, all members of the
community are inextricably bound together.

DETRITUS

BEACH WRACK

FOURTH
ORDER
CONSUMER

ONE POUND

THIRD
ORDER
CONSUMERS

10 POUNDS

SECOND
ORDER
CONSUMERS

100 POUNDS

FIRST
ORDER
(PRIMARY)
CONSUMERS

1,000 POUNDS

PRODUCERS

10,000
POUNDS

To gain one pound, a seal (fourth-order consumer) must eat the equivalent of 10,000 pounds of planktonic plants (producers). The drastic decline in the amount of energy (weight) at each level occurs because living things do not convert more than a fraction of their food into living tissue. Approximately 90 per cent of the energy is lost with each transfer along the food chain.

simply states that there are fewer and fewer high-order consumers (carnivores) as the food chain becomes farther removed from plants. You should have no trouble finding examples. In an area of a few square yards or in a tide pool, which are more abundant, small grazing shrimp or large predatory fish?

Man comes to the shore

How many beaches or rocky shores do you know where there are no people, no houses, no factories, no vessels? The seashore, with its beauty, its advantages for recreation and transportation, has become some of the most sought-after real estate. If you can find a strip of virgin shore, enjoy it to its fullest, for when you return in a few years it may no longer be the same. We have to use the shore in our civilization, but we do not always use it wisely.

Although the seas cover 70 per cent of the earth's surface, man prefers to farm the land. We obtain food from less than 1 per cent of the ocean's total production. It is time we learned about the possibilities for more extensive development of the seacoast and shallow seas.

Fish, for instance, could be farmed. They respond well to being fed and generally stay in areas that are favorable for food and shelter. Marine scientists are experimenting with artificial reefs in the form of cement pipe, sunken automobile wrecks, and even old trolley cars as refuges for fish and the animals they eat. Fish populations in such spots increase dramatically.

Although in the United States we can almost all obtain fresh, canned, or frozen fish, there is another, much cheaper, way in which fish could be used to feed the world's underfed people. Fish are a rich source of the protein desperately needed by more than a billion people. Ground up and purified, fish become a wholesome flour that can be used in many ways. Other types of processing yield fertilizer, oils, paint bases, minerals, vitamins, animal foods, and a variety of other products.

Botanists are interested in the culture of certain forms of

Gulls hover overhead, waiting to pilfer a few strays, while a group of California fishermen haul in a net full of herring on Tomales Bay.

algae, some of which are marine. Experimental algal culture is already being tried in several parts of the world. In many countries seaweeds are important additions to human diet, although in the Western world we seldom eat them.

A great many shoreline animals other than fish, crabs, lobsters, clams, and oysters are edible. Elsewhere people eat sea urchins, sea cucumbers, conches, mussels, Palolo worms, octopus, squid, skates, and a legion of other animals from the sea. We may limit ourselves to only a few types of seafood, but our shores abound with more good eating than can be imagined—if only we have the courage to try a novelty!

The eventual proper utilization of shore and coastal resources can bring work for many. Not all our marine-life industries are in a good economic condition today, too often because we do not understand the biology of marine organisms. Our lobster, crab, oyster, clam, and scallop fisheries have suffered and are in need of increased protection and control.

Mistakes we have made

In many areas coastal fish and other animals mentioned above have simply been overfished. Nets, traps, and dredges used in the same region year after year either eliminate animals from the area or cause them to migrate elsewhere. Many populations and communities have become so depleted they may never recover, even if left completely alone for many years.

Salt marshes, so amazingly productive (but "wastelands" to some development engineers) are being drained, filled in, or otherwise obliterated at an alarming rate. This seriously decreases the flow of nutrients to coastal waters, but the precise effects often are difficult to measure and may take a long time to become apparent. Pollution can be cured, but an alteration of a salt marsh is permanent. When the true worth of the marshes to the biological economy of the seas is finally realized, nothing can be done to bring them back.

A bulging net full of ocean trout is hoisted aboard a commercial fishing boat. Once nets were lowered on a hit-or-miss basis, but nowadays many trawlers are equipped with "fish scopes," sonar devices that enable fishermen to locate and follow schools of fish.

Highly productive marsh grass provides a continuing supply of nutrients to other forms of life, both in the marsh and in the neighboring coastal water. When a salt marsh is filled in with debris (as the marsh shown here is being filled in), this crucial source of nourishment is destroyed forever.

Neglect as well as overuse can kill shore organisms. Human destruction of cover vegetation on land, with resulting erosion, often brings floods that carry quantities of sediment from the land out to sea. Sediment suspended in river water cuts down the light in previously clear coastal water, preventing plant production. Sediment also settles on the bottom in thick blankets, suffocating animals that cannot escape. In addition, floods of fresh water from eroded land flow in great sheets over the denser salt water of bays and shallow seas, killing a great many sessile marine organisms living a foot or more below low tide. While it is not always obvious, man's destructiveness far inland can result in widespread disaster for marine life hundreds of miles away.

When fire or bulldozing destroys cover vegetation on beaches and capes, the sand is blown inland and streams across fertile fields, destroying crops and homes. Great sand waves have been recorded in Maine, Massachusetts, Delaware, Virginia, and California, and lesser ones occur on every sandy coast.

Intertidal and subtidal sand can move as well. When

bottom populations are killed off, their anchoring effect is lost, or when channels are dredged and inlets cut through, quantities of bottom sand may drift with tides and currents to new locations. Some regions then build up quickly, while others are depleted of sand—sandbars rise to the surface, and whole beaches disappear. Thorough study of a coastline by marine engineers and oceanographers will show how these effects can be avoided, yet too often uninformed local authorities, who do not want to spend a few dollars to hire experts, construct jetties and breakwaters which do almost exactly what they are supposed to prevent. Expertly placed walls known as *groins* preserve beaches and allow them to build at a healthy rate. Fine examples of this kind of planning are found along parts of the California coast.

Some of our shoreline disappears forever under shore resorts and cities. Except for the beachfront itself, there is nothing left of the large barrier island now occupied by Miami Beach. Developments of this sort are necessary for our expanding population, but do all our shorelines have such a fate in store for them?

Unquestionably the most serious effect man has had on the seashore, as well as on fresh-water resources, could easily be prevented—*pollution*.

There are many kinds of pollution, from a wide variety of substances released into rivers and into the ocean itself. Domestic wastes, sewage, and industrial wastes have been

Only by constructing a sturdy sea wall was it possible to build a highway along this wave-battered strip of California coast. Efforts to counteract the power of the waves are not always so successful.

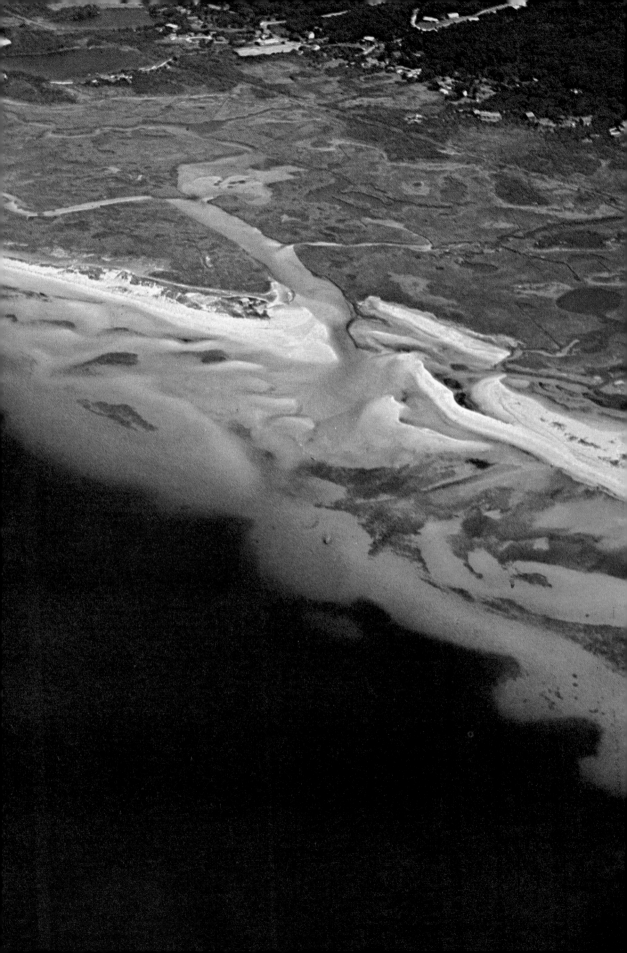

flowing out to sea for more than a century, often completely altering the populations and communities of bays and shores. In the eighteenth century, for example, the Raritan River Valley in New Jersey was so pleasant that George Washington considered settling there. Yet from the 1920s until a few years ago the river had been so polluted that the only living things it contained were bacteria and a few insect larvae. Fumes from the river, which became an open sewer, turned white houses dark and peeled paint from buildings. Raritan Bay oysters were once famous in New York restaurants, but they have vanished; the few that remain are unsafe to eat.

Given a chance, a river can recover. Recently, worried residents and industries along the Raritan have begun to cooperate in preventing pollution. Fish are already appearing in the river, some many miles upstream, and are being caught by fishermen in localities where no fish had been seen for nearly half a century. Raritan Bay is beginning to have increased populations of swimming and attached marine animals. Adjacent bay and coastal shorelines should recover quickly after the river has been cleaned up, if it is kept clean.

One result of oil carelessly spilled on coastal water— a crab tarred and feathered with crude oil and sand.

Some of the effects of industries on coastal waters are accidental. When shoreline refineries pump oil into ships, there may be serious spillage, which, of course, is costly to the oil companies. But such accidents are costly in other ways as well: the oil, lighter than water, spreads for many miles over marshes, bays, and beaches, trapping and killing enormous numbers of waterfowl, shore birds, crabs, fish, and other creatures. Some industries pipe in bay water for cooling purposes, then release it. While the water is not polluted, the slight rise in temperature can profoundly affect the settling of larvae and the migration of young fish.

Pesticides—valuable or harmful?

Another grave concern is that of pesticides. Much has been written about both sides of this issue. Without doubt pesticides control many destructive insect pests, thereby increas-

An aerial view reveals the handiwork of tides and currents that relentlessly transport the coastal sand. The shifting pattern beneath the water at the edge of this tidal marsh on Cape Cod is a series of intertidal dunes and submerged sandbars.

Each year many bald eagle eggs fail to hatch. Scientists suspect that the culprit may be DDT, which passes up the food chain to the fish eaten by the eagles. Traces of the pesticide have been found in some of the unhatched eggs.

ing crop yield and preventing disease. But there is also little doubt that wide use of pesticides can seriously alter the ecological balance of a region, and not just on land. Many of these chemical preparations are remarkably stable and do not disintegrate easily. They wash down rivers and out to sea, where they poison many sensitive forms of life.

People who propose wider use of pesticides demand proof that they harm natural populations. Those who oppose widespread use of these chemicals know that such proof often is a long time in coming. There may be subtle changes in a community because only one or two members are affected at first. Finally, though, the total community structure may change radically and even disappear.

Because many pesticides are stable they travel far, doing damage over and over. An animal that takes them in and sickens or dies may be eaten by a scavenger, which passes on the poisons to the next consumer. At the end of a food chain the final consumer may accumulate too much of the chemical and die. Or an animal carrying the poison may distribute a particularly dangerous compound far beyond the region for which it was intended.

Some effects are rapid. For example, many crustaceans, primarily the larval forms, are killed by pesticides used for insects. One summer a local mosquito-control group sprayed several thousand acres of salt marsh, killing the mosquitoes that had been seriously bothering nearby residential areas. Within days the outgoing flood tides in marsh creeks carried hundreds of thousands of young crabs, dead and dying, to

196

the sea. Had the pesticide killed them? Were other compounds available that would have destroyed the mosquitoes but not the crabs? Had anyone thought of crab populations in the salt marshes? Did anyone care?

Perhaps the most important lesson to be learned from such examples is to act cautiously. Of course, we can never foresee every possibility, but usually we plunge into matters of life and death for the natural economy knowing and caring little about the possible widespread effects of our actions. Well-documented disasters abound throughout our history, especially in our land resources—forests, wildlife, lakes, rivers, and the like. But are the seas and their coasts inexhaustible? It would be worth your while to go out of your way to see a thoroughly polluted bay, or a beach covered with crude oil in which birds, intertidal animals, and fish are trapped and dead. Afterward you will not be able to assume that shorelines and their populations can take care of themselves when man is careless. Man now has the ability to use, improve, or destroy every world environment, including the seashore.

Oil spilled on nearby water eventually accumulated on the beaches of these islands off southern Florida, staining them with a suffocating blanket that brought death to many shore animals.

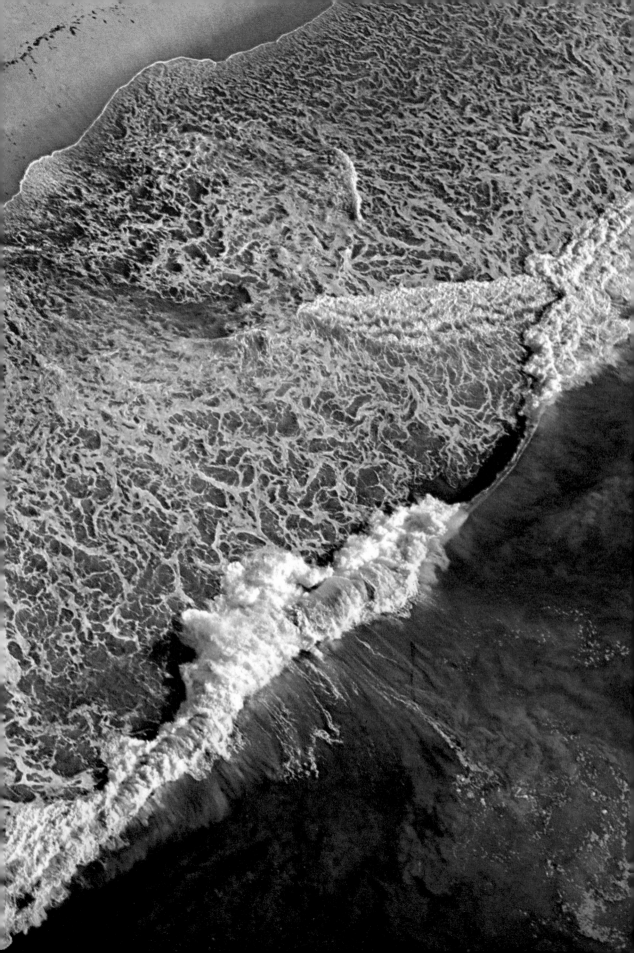

The world of the seashore

The seashore, the great meeting place of the world of land and the world of water, has many riches to reveal to the visitor who really wants to see. To some a beach is merely a place to swim and lie in the sun; a rocky coast may be only a vantage point from which to watch foam and crashing waves, and to feel the strength of the sea wind. To others, a salt marsh is a place on which to construct a blind for shooting migrating waterfowl. Coral beaches may be no more than fine hunting grounds for the shell collector. But for the person with curiosity and an active mind, any shore provides unlimited adventure.

There is more to the seashore than its obvious pleasures. Once you recognize its heavy populations of seaweeds, marsh plants, and animals, you have begun to appreciate it. What goes unseen by most shore visitors is the enormous "base" for life provided in shallow water and intertidal areas—the trapping of solar energy by microscopic algae and salt-marsh grasses. Then there is the fascination of unraveling the puzzles of energy transfer from one life form to the next, and the gradual understanding of complex plant and animal relationships.

Perhaps because we are creatures of the land, it seems that the strangest forms of life on earth live in the sea. Many of them are close at hand in tide pools and in burrows beneath our feet. Here, indeed, one can enter a different world without traveling to another planet. Yet this marine world is, after all, a vital part of our own existence and will become more and more important as human beings increase in number and exhaust resources on land. We need to learn as much as we can, for with only partial and imperfect understanding, mankind often affects shore life adversely—and ultimately to his detriment. Properly managed, the seashore can be one of humanity's greatest resources. Properly preserved, it will remain the exciting frontier between two worlds and our gateway to the sea.

Surging breakers spread an apron of foam across the shifting frontier between land and sea, the scene of an endless and exciting drama visible to all who take the time to look.

Appendix

Seashore Areas in the National Park System

Dotting the coastline of the United States is a chain of National Parks, Monuments, and Seashores—areas of unique scenic, scientific, and recreational value that have been set aside for the enjoyment of all the people. In the face of burgeoning demands for open space, their value increases year by year; they are practically the only wild, uninhabited natural areas of any size remaining along our coasts. Here, unhampered by no-trespassing signs, Americans can observe and enjoy the sea, the shore, and all that lives there. They can roam along beaches uncluttered by buildings, fences, or other signs of civilization. They can camp, swim, picnic, fish, hike, or simply sit and watch the waves. They can visit interpretive exhibits and museums, travel the marked nature trails, or join guided walks and lecture programs led by professional naturalists. Best of all, the National Parks, Monuments, and Seashores are places where city-bred Americans can find solitude and the refreshment of spirit that comes of contact with wilderness and open spaces.

Outstanding features of major seashore units in the National Park System are described here. The National Parks and Monuments were created primarily as living museums to preserve unique remnants of America's outdoor heritage. Even so, recreational use of these national treasures is encouraged insofar as it does not impair their value as scenic and scientific reserves. National Seashores, on the other hand, are mainly recreational areas. Here too an important objective is the preservation of scenic stretches of wild, undeveloped beach as a legacy to be passed on for the enjoyment of future generations.

ANGEL-WING CLAM SHELLS

Acadia National Park (Maine)

Includes parts of Mount Desert Island, nearby Schoodic Peninsula, and Isle au Haut. Noted for its superbly scenic rocky coast, including wave-carved cliffs, caves, and natural sea walls; foaming surf; hundreds of tide pools; variety of sea birds. In the background, rugged forest-covered mountains rise abruptly from the sea. See pages 94–95.

Assateague Island National Seashore (Maryland, Virginia)

A slender barrier island on the Middle Atlantic coast, within easy traveling distance for millions of people. Broad, gently sloping sandy beaches on the ocean side, extensive marshes on the bay side. Includes Chincoteague National Wildlife Refuge, winter home for a remarkable variety of waterfowl, including swans. Also roaming the island is the famous herd of wild Chincoteague ponies. Like all barrier islands, this is a fragile, constantly changing landscape; part of the shoreline has migrated at least 1000 feet to the west in the last thirty years. There is dramatic evidence of shoreline migration in areas where a 1962 storm exposed large cedar stumps along the foreshore—remnants of a forest that once grew along what was then the edge of the bay.

Buck Island Reef National Monument (Virgin Islands)

One of the finest marine gardens in the Caribbean. Mile-long Buck Island, off the coast of St. Croix, is fringed by a magnificent barrier reef; a lavish array of corals, sea fans, gorgonians, colorful fishes, and molluscs flourishes beneath the brilliantly clear water. Other attractions are the island's large rookery of frigate birds and occasional sightings of hawksbill and green turtles. Chartered boats from nearby St. Croix transport visitors to this underwater paradise.

Cabrillo National Monument (California)

Primarily a historical monument commemorating discovery of the California coast by Juan Rodríguez Cabrillo in 1542; lies at the tip of Point Loma on San Diego Bay. The sandy shores surrounding parts of the Point are one of many spawning areas for the famed California grunion. See page 31.

Cape Cod National Seashore (Massachusetts)

Preserves large portions of this historic peninsula for public enjoyment. Broad beaches, rolling dunes, tall cliffs, woodlands, fresh-water ponds, and extensive fresh- and salt-water marshes in a landscape dotted by picturesque villages. Camping nearby, plus fishing, swimming, and interpretive exhibits and programs in an area that has long been a favorite with vacationers. See pages 76–77 and 118.

BRAIN CORAL

Cape Hatteras National Seashore (North Carolina)

A chain of barrier islands extending for seventy miles along the Carolina coast, in places as much as thirty miles from the mainland. Broad deserted beaches, shifting dunes, magnificent surf, and pleasant villages lend a special charm. Excellent sport fishing; abundant birdlife, especially at Pea Island National Wildlife Refuge; Atlantic bottle-nosed dolphins sometimes sighted within yards of shore. Diamond Shoals, an area of dangerous shallows off the tip of the Cape, has earned the forbidding name of "graveyard of the Atlantic"; remains of ships wrecked long ago still dot the coastline.

Channel Islands National Monument (California)

Includes Santa Barbara and Anacapa, two small but spectacular islands off the coast of southern California. Girdled by almost-vertical cliffs (in places more than 500 feet high), these rugged, seldom-visited islands provide refuge for huge nesting colonies of sea birds and an exceptional variety of marine mammals. Besides sea lions and sea elephants, visitors now and then spot a sea otter and the rare Guadalupe fur seal. Because of long isolation from the mainland, the islands also harbor an assortment of distinctive plants, including the world's largest single stand of giant coreopsis, an unusual treelike sunflower.

Everglades National Park (Florida)

The largest remaining subtropical wilderness in the United States, including both land areas and many small islands in the adjacent Gulf of Mexico and Florida Bay. Along the coast are thousands of acres of dense mangrove forest interlaced by a maze of waterways. Rare and colorful birdlife includes egrets, herons, ibises, roseate spoonbills, pelicans, cormorants, and many more. Other prime attractions are manatees, alligators, and crocodiles, as well as the loggerhead turtles that come ashore to lay their eggs at Cape Sable. See pages 132–133.

AMERICAN CROCODILE

Fire Island National Seashore (New York)

A long, largely undeveloped gem of a barrier island off the southern shore of Long Island. Particularly valuable for public recreation because of its location; nearly one third of the nation's population lives within a day's drive. Firm beaches, dunes, salt marshes, and varied plant life, including a stand of virgin holly trees several hundred years old (the Sunken Forest). Plans for developing the area (established in 1964) emphasize preservation of long stretches of undisturbed wild beach.

Fort Jefferson National Monument (Florida)

Includes seven small coral islands (the Dry Tortugas) and about seventy-five square miles of surrounding shoals and water in the Gulf of Mexico west of the Florida Keys. The central feature is the ruin of a large century-old fort, but the real attraction at these semitropical islands is their bird and marine life. Beneath the warm shallow water are extensive coral reefs teeming with tropical fishes and a host of other animals and plants. Besides a rookery of about 120,000 sooty terns and several hundred noddy terns, as many as 200 frigate birds gather here each summer, along with boobies, gulls, roseate terns, and many others.

Olympic National Park *(Washington)*

The seashore area of this famed mountain park includes a rugged, fifty-mile-long strip of the Pacific coast. With many areas accessible only on foot, the Olympic coast is one of the most unspoiled remaining in the United States. Sandy beaches, rocky cliffs, tide pools, and many offshore islands frequented by seals and sea birds make this a supremely varied and scenic seashore. See pages 104–105.

QUEEN CONCH

Padre Island National Seashore *(Texas)*

Eighty miles of uninhabited seashore on a barrier island that arches along the Gulf coast just north of Mexico; the longest undeveloped beach remaining in the contiguous United States. Noted for its pleasant climate, broad sandy beaches, dunes up to forty feet high, abundance of shells, excellent surf fishing, varied birdlife. In addition to huge flocks of wintering waterfowl, birds include herons, terns, egrets, brown pelicans, white pelicans, an occasional frigate bird, and many more. Padre Island's finest quality is solitude and the opportunity to observe and enjoy the sea, the shore, and wildlife in an area untouched by civilization.

Point Reyes National Seashore *(California)*

A beautiful peninsula north of San Francisco. The forested ridges and rolling grasslands of the interior are bordered by long, broad beaches backed by tall palisadelike cliffs. Large resident herd of sea lions; colonies of sea birds on offshore rocks; sheltered lagoons; rolling dunes; magnificent vistas of the Pacific from windswept bluffs. See pages 82–83.

Virgin Islands National Park *(Virgin Islands)*

A tropical island park in the Caribbean east of Puerto Rico; includes about two thirds of St. John, smallest of the three principal United States Virgin Islands. Steep mountains and valleys covered with tropical vegetation; ruins of colonial sugar plantations; relics of pre-Columbian Indians; white sandy beaches; extensive offshore coral reefs teeming with colorful corals, sponges, fishes, and other animals. The self-guiding underwater nature trail at Trunk Bay offers an especially rewarding experience for snorkelers and underwater photographers.

CANADA

OLYMPIC NAT'L. PK.

WASH.

WATERTON-GLACIER INTERNATIONAL PEACE PK.

MT. RAINIER NAT'L. PK.

GLACIER NAT'L. PK.

WHITMAN NAT'L. MON.

MONTANA

THEODORE ROOSEVELT NAT'L. MEM. PK.

N. DAK.

OREGON

CRATER LAKE NAT'L. PK.

LAVA BEDS NAT'L. MON.

IDAHO

DEVIL'S TOWER NAT'L. MON.

YELLOWSTONE NAT'L. PK.

SOUTH DAK.

OREGON CAVES NAT'L. MON.

CRATERS OF THE MOON NAT'L. MON.

WYOMING

WIND CAVE NAT'L. PK.

BADLANDS NAT'L. MON.

LASSEN VOLCANIC NAT'L. PK.

GRAND TETON NAT'L. PK.

FORT LARAMIE NAT'L. MON.

POINT REYES NAT'L. SEASHORE

NEVADA

UTAH

TIMPANOGOS CAVE NAT'L. MON.

DINOSAUR NAT'L. MON.

SCOTT'S BLUFF NAT'L. MON.

MUIR WOODS NAT'L. MON.

LEHMAN CAVES NAT'L. MON.

CAPITOL REEF NAT'L. MON.

COLORADO NAT'L. MON.

ROCKY MOUNTAIN NAT'L. PK.

NEBRAS

CALIF.

DEVIL'S POSTPILE NAT'L. MON.

BRYCE CANYON NAT'L. PK.

ARCHES NAT'L. MON.

YOSEMITE NAT'L. PK.

PINNACLES NAT'L. MON.

SEQUOIA AND KINGS CANYON NAT'L. PKS.

CEDAR BREAKS NAT'L. MON.

NAVAJO NAT'L. MON.

CANYONLANDS NAT'L. PK.

COLO.

BLACK CANYON OF THE GUNNISON NAT'L. MON.

KANSAS

ZION NAT'L. PK.

NATURAL BRIDGES NAT'L. MON.

GREAT SAND DUNES NAT'L. MON.

DEATH VALLEY NAT'L. MON.

RAINBOW BRIDGE NAT'L. MON.

MESA VERDE NAT'L. PK.

CHACO CANYON NAT'L. MON.

LAKE MEAD NAT'L. RECREATION AREA

WUPATKI NAT'L. MON.

CHANNEL ISLANDS NAT'L. MON.

JOSHUA TREE NAT'L. MON.

GRAND CANYON NAT'L. PK. AND MON.

SUNSET CRATER NAT'L. MON.

AZTEC RUINS NAT'L. MON.

CAPULIN MT. NAT'L. MON.

CANYON DE CHELLY NAT'L. MON.

OK

CABRILLO NAT'L. MON.

ARIZ.

TUZIGOOT NAT'L. MON.

PETRIFIED FOREST NAT'L. MON.

WALNUT CANYON NAT'L. MON.

BANDELIER NAT'L. MON.

PLA
NAT

ORGAN PIPE CACTUS NAT'L. MON.

MONTEZUMA CASTLE NAT'L. MON.

CASA GRANDE NAT'L. MON.

WHITE SANDS NAT'L. MON.

SAGUARO NAT'L. MON.

NEW MEX.

ALASKA

MT. McKINLEY NAT'L. PK.

CANADA

CHIRICAHUA NAT'L. MON.

CARLSBAD CAVERNS NAT'L. MON.

TEXA

KATMAI NAT'L. MON.

GLACIER BAY NAT'L. MON.

MEXICO

BIG BEND NAT'L. PK.

0   100 MILES

HAWAII

0   50 MILES

HALEAKALA NAT'L. PK.

CITY OF REFUGE NAT'L. HISTORICAL PK.

HAWAII NAT'L. PK.

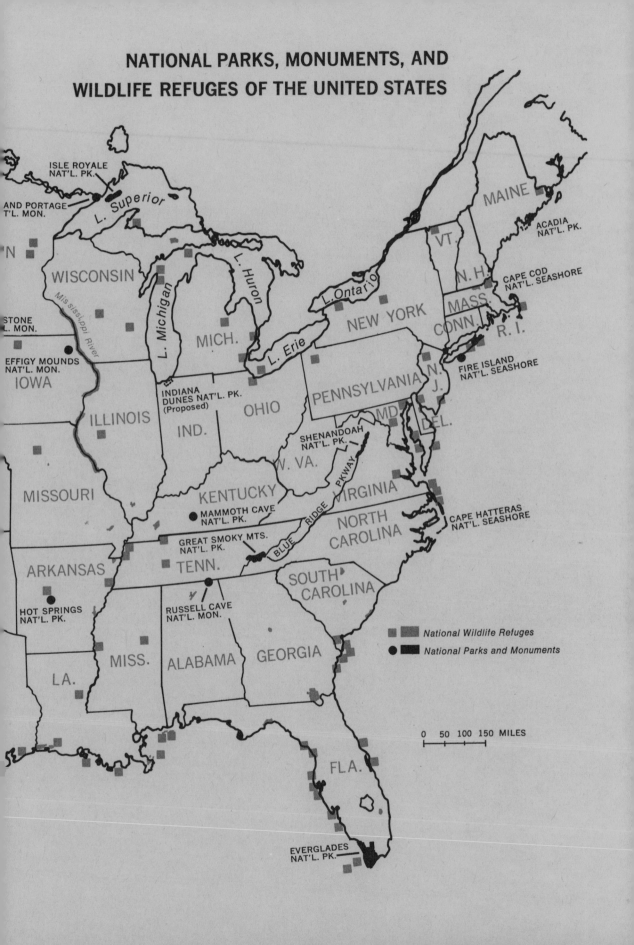

NATIONAL PARKS, MONUMENTS, AND
WILDLIFE REFUGES OF THE UNITED STATES

ISLE ROYALE
NAT'L. PK.

AND PORTAGE
T'L. MON.

L. Superior

N

WISCONSIN

L. Michigan

L. Huron

MICH.

STONE
L. MON.

Mississippi River

EFFIGY MOUNDS
NAT'L. MON.

IOWA

ILLINOIS

IND.

INDIANA
DUNES NAT'L. PK.
(Proposed)

OHIO

L. Erie

L. Ontario

NEW YORK

MAINE

VT.

N. H.

ACADIA
NAT'L. PK.

CAPE COD
NAT'L. SEASHORE

MASS.

CONN.

R. I.

PENNSYLVANIA

N.
J.

FIRE ISLAND
NAT'L. SEASHORE

MD.

DEL.

SHENANDOAH
NAT'L. PK.

W. VA.

PKWAY

MISSOURI

KENTUCKY

MAMMOTH CAVE
NAT'L. PK.

VIRGINIA

BLUE

RIDGE

NORTH
CAROLINA

CAPE HATTERAS
NAT'L. SEASHORE

GREAT SMOKY MTS.
NAT'L. PK.

ARKANSAS

TENN.

SOUTH
CAROLINA

HOT SPRINGS
NAT'L. PK.

RUSSELL CAVE
NAT'L. MON.

MISS.

ALABAMA

GEORGIA

LA.

National Wildlife Refuges

National Parks and Monuments

0   50 100 150 MILES

FLA.

EVERGLADES
NAT'L. PK.

National Wildlife Refuges

Scattered across the United States is a system of nearly 300 National Wildlife Refuges managed by the Department of the Interior. These farflung areas preserve vitally needed open space where a great variety of birds and animals can feed, rest, and raise their young. Many are located on the seacoast, primarily for the benefit of migratory waterfowl. They provide both wintering areas and places where birds can stop for food and rest during their spring and fall migrations.

Although they were acquired primarily for wildlife, portions of many refuges are open for public recreation. Thousands of visitors flock to the coastal refuges each year simply to watch the spectacle of the birds. Others use the seashores for swimming, fishing, picnicking, hiking, or nature study. A few refuges even include some primitive camping facilities. Human use of the areas of course must be limited lest their value to wildlife be impaired. Even so, many of the refuges offer fine opportunities to observe the life of the seashore. Major attractions at several coastal National Wildlife Refuges are described here. Location of others is shown on the map on pages 206–207.

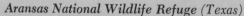

Aransas National Wildlife Refuge (Texas)
A 47,000-acre refuge on the Texas Gulf coast, including wooded and grassy uplands and extensive coastal marshes, was secured in 1937. Prize attraction is the wintering flock of famous whooping cranes, one of America's largest and rarest birds. During the winter all of these cranes remaining in the world—less than fifty—are on this refuge. To avoid disturbing the wary cranes, visitors must watch them only from an observation tower near the edge of their territory or from a boat in the Intercoastal Waterway. Winter browse has been provided for the cranes within fenced fields. Nearly 300 species of birds have been recorded at this important way station and wintering ground, including thousands of ducks, geese, and sandbill cranes. Herons, egrets, roseate spoonbills, and many shore birds are resident on the refuge. The resident populations of deer, javelina (collared peccary), armadillo, and other mammals have been steadily increasing.

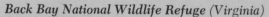

Back Bay National Wildlife Refuge (Virginia)
An isolated 9000-acre refuge on the Virginia coast southeast of Norfolk was acquired in 1938. There are sandy barrier beaches,

WHOOPING CRANE

fresh- and salt-water marshes, and extensive areas of open water. Fields are cultivated to provide winter browse for the thousands of geese that visit the area. Although the refuge is accessible only by water or by several miles of beach driving, several thousand visitors arrive each year to birdwatch, fish, swim, picnic, and enjoy the solitude. Most spectacular of the 250 or more species of birds recorded here are wintering concentrations of whistling swans, Canada and snow geese, innumerable ducks, and other shore and water birds. At times this refuge and nearby Mackay Island National Wildlife Refuge provide food and protection for the entire world population of greater snow geese, which nest on Greenland and other islands within the Arctic Circle. Experiments are being conducted to determine the effect of increased saline waters on the tremendous beds of submerged aquatics that provide food for ducks. The results of these studies will be important along the entire Atlantic coast.

SNOW GEESE

Brigantine National Wildlife Refuge (New Jersey)
A 15,000-acre refuge was established in 1939 on the heavily populated New Jersey coast just north of Atlantic City. The terrain is primarily cordgrass-saltgrass tidal marsh interspersed with tidal bays and channels. Two huge fresh-water pools have been constructed by diking, a project requiring considerable time and expense. Foods attractive to ducks and geese are grown, and several species have remained to nest. The unparalleled opportunity for bird watchers to drive around the dikes and study the birds at leisure makes this one of the finest spots for bird watching along the entire Atlantic coast. Winter waterfowl populations normally surpass 150,000 birds, especially brant and black duck. Holgate Peninsula, a smaller area nearby, is managed as part of the refuge and provides exceptional habitat for a number of nesting and migrant birds.

Chassahowitzka National Wildlife Refuge (Florida)
This 28,000-acre refuge on the Gulf Coast, 65 miles north of St. Petersburg, was purchased in 1943. Terrain ranges from dry sandhills to nearly impenetrable hardwood swamps, salt-water marshes, and countless mangrove keys checkered by a network of streams, bays, rivers, and bayous. The refuge attracts wintering ducks, rails, gallinules, loons, and pelicans; summer nesting colonies of thousands of cormorants; and a great variety of herons and egrets, ospreys, a few ibises, and many other species. There are also alligators, otters, mink, deer, raccoons, bears, bobcats, panthers, and many other animals. The aquatic foods are supplemented with cultivated browse to attract geese further south in Florida.

Chincoteague National Wildlife Refuge (Virginia, Maryland)
This fine 9460-acre seashore wilderness on the Middle Atlantic

coast, including all land south of the Maryland line, was acquired in 1943. Through the construction of fresh-water pools, it has developed into the most important waterfowl area between Bombay Hook National Wildlife Refuge, Delaware, on the north and Back Bay National Wildlife Refuge, Virginia, on the south. It is part of Assateague Island National Seashore (see pages 202–203). Dunes on the ocean side of the island protect the fresh-water pools. There are salt marshes on the bay side and a large wooded area near the southern tip. This refuge is the most important resting and feeding ground for migrating shore birds and wintering waterfowl, including at times most of the world population of greater snow geese, brant, and a few whistling swans. It also provides a home for exotic sika deer and a herd of wild Chincoteague ponies. The shallow waters of the bay are a famed shell-fishing area.

Monomoy National Wildlife Refuge (Massachusetts)
The ten-mile-long sandspit of 2700 acres stretching south from the elbow of Cape Cod was secured in 1944. It is bounded on the east by the open Atlantic, on the west by Nantucket Sound. Terrain includes sandy shores and dunes, salt marsh, fresh-water ponds and marshes, and a small but dense woodland of scrubby pines and underbrush. More than 300 species of birds, including 35 kinds of shore birds, have been recorded, especially during migration periods. In fall and winter as many as a million eiders and scoters use the surrounding water areas. Most of this renowned refuge is accessible only by water, but thousands of visitors come each year for bird watching, nature study, shell collecting, picnicking, hiking, fishing, and photography.

Parker River National Wildlife Refuge (Massachusetts)
This 6400-acre refuge on the Atlantic, 35 miles north of Boston, was acquired in 1945 primarily as a concentration area for Canada geese and black ducks. It has been very successful in attracting more than 300 different kinds of birds, including waterfowl. Terns and shore birds are among the nesting birds using the beaches and marshes. The refuge is a picturesque combination of dunes, thickets, marshes, and tidal flats bounded by six miles of sandy beach. The diversity of habitats supports abundant and varied plant and animal life. A recreation area with access to the superb ocean beach is open to the public, but entry to other areas of the refuge requires special permission. In addition to recreational activities such as swimming, surf fishing, nature study, and photography, visitors can obtain permits for clamdigging and picking the plentiful beach plums and cranberries. Special deer hunts have been held when surpluses need to be reduced. The number of visitors now exceeds a quarter million persons annually.

210

Pea Island National Wildlife Refuge (North Carolina)

This 5880-acre refuge on the Outer Banks, 30 miles north of Cape Hatteras, was purchased in 1938. The thirteen miles of barrier island on the Atlantic coast are part of Cape Hatteras National Seashore (see page 203). Pea Island is a major terminal wintering area for the greater snow goose, Canada geese, brant, and other waterfowl. It has the only large concentration of gadwall nesting on the Atlantic seaboard; there are also royal terns, black skimmers, gulls, egrets, herons, and others in summer. The success of this refuge in attracting thousands of ducks, geese, gulls, terns, and shore birds resulted from the construction of fresh-water ponds for the production of aquatic foods. Bird-observation platforms are provided, and other recreational uses are encouraged, including camping in an area at the northern tip of the island, beachcombing on the broad sandy beaches, and excellent surf casting, especially for channel bass.

Willapa National Wildlife Refuge (Washington)

This major Pacific-coast wintering area of 8175 acres was established in 1937 for black brant, Canada geese, and other water birds. The refuge is on Willapa Bay, has an additional 10,000 acres of surrounding water closed to hunting by Presidential Proclamation, and contains several fresh-water springs. Limited archery hunting for black bear and mule deer is sometimes permitted. The manager of this area is also responsible for several small island refuges off the Pacific coast of Washington and Oregon and in Washington's Puget Sound. These islands provide some of the best nesting areas for auklets, petrels, tufted puffins, murres, guillemots, cormorants, and other sea birds.

BLACK SKIMMER

Vanishing Animals of the Seashore

In a sense many animals of the seashore are in danger, for their habitat is being damaged or destroyed with alarming speed along much of our coastline. Industrial wastes, raw sewage, and pesticidal residues contaminate our waters, killing many animals outright and transforming others into carriers of dangerous diseases and toxic chemicals. Great expanses of wild shoreline are swallowed up each year by housing developments, factories, and motels. Salt marshes are recklessly drained or filled with garbage. With the destruction of each bit of habitat, a whole community of life disappears forever from the area.

Human interference of this sort affects some animals more than others. Marine invertebrates seldom are threatened with complete extinction. Most are abundant and reproduce in enormous numbers. If their habitat is ruined in one place, they may continue to flourish

BALD EAGLE

Even America's national bird is fighting a losing battle to survive; the bald eagle remains abundant only in Alaska. Each year fewer and fewer eagle eggs are hatching. Scientists have discovered DDT in the embryos inside unhatched eggs and suspect that the poison may be responsible for their failure to hatch. Contaminated eggs result from a chain of events that begins when man douses the landscape with insecticides. Without losing any of their potency, the poisons drain into streams and coastal waters, passing along food chains to fish and finally to eagles when they eat the fish. Researchers now are trying to determine whether or not DDT is indeed the cause of the drastic decline in eagle reproduction all over the continental United States. They fear the worst.

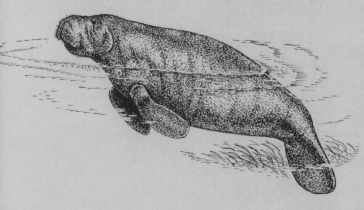

MANATEE

A mammal whose ancestors long ago returned to the water, the manatee is well adapted for life in shallow fresh- or salt-water bays and rivers, where it feeds on eelgrass, water hyacinths, and other aquatic plants. Never abundant, it still is seen occasionally along the Gulf coast and the east coast of Florida. Although these shy, ungainly animals are protected by law in Florida, some thoughtless boaters still regard them merely as targets and shoot at the few remaining manatees as they come to the surface for an occasional gulp of air.

elsewhere; and if conditions improve, they are quick to recolonize a habitat. Aerial or land-dwelling vertebrates, on the other hand, cannot stand as much interference and persecution; their numbers are fewer to begin with, and in general they produce fewer young. Pictured here are four vertebrates, often associated with the seashore, whose plights are especially critical.

Although the solutions are costly, the problems facing the wildlife of our seashores can be solved. More areas such as our National Parks and Wildlife Refuges must be set aside. Pollution must be brought under control regardless of cost. But most of all, we must learn to manage our resources more wisely. Once destroyed, the wildlife heritage that is ours to pass on to future generations cannot be replaced.

OSPREY

At any seashore or inland lake you visit, you may be lucky enough to glimpse the fish hawk soaring high above the water. Much bolder than most other hawks, the fish-eating osprey often nests near man, sometimes in loose colonies of a hundred birds or more. But more and more often in recent years, incubating ospreys wait in vain for their eggs to hatch. As in the case of the bald eagle, scientists suspect that DDT is the culprit. This beautiful harmless hawk can be saved, but only if all people develop more responsible attitudes toward the community of living things.

ESKIMO CURLEW

Once the Eskimo curlew was so plentiful that huge flocks of migrants could be seen in the spring and fall; today even a fleeting glimpse of this handsome shore bird is cause for renewed hope that a few may yet survive. Their decrease resulted purely from human greed. All along their northward migration route up the Mississippi Valley, bands of market hunters used to shoot them by the wagonload to sell for food. The slaughter was so thorough that the Eskimo curlew was all but extinct by 1925. Hope that a few still survived to breed recurred periodically when a few birds were seen from time to time along the Texas coast. But on September 4, 1963, a hunter shot a lone curlew on the Caribbean island of Barbados. Could it have been that this was the last surviving Eskimo curlew? Only time will tell.

Major Groups of Seashore Animals

PROTOZOAN (*Foraminifera*)

Protozoa—Single-cell Animals

Minute single-cell protozoans exist by the millions in sea water. The most ancient of all animal groups, they include some forms (dinoflagellates) that possess both plant and animal characteristics. Although protozoans generally are regarded as primitive, they are by no means simple; the single cell is able to carry on all the complex functions of life. Extremely varied and sometimes even bizarre in form, different species may be cloaked with minute cilia or equipped with whiplike flagella or sucking tentacles. Some are relatively formless specks of protoplasm, while others are encased in elaborate shells of lime or silica.

SPONGE (*Deadman's Fingers*)

Porifera—Sponges

Sponges are the simplest of the many-cell animals. Perforated by thousands of pores, canals, and inner chambers, they are little more than living sieves. Unable to move from place to place, sponges extract food from streams of water that are pumped through their bodies by the constant beating of microscopic hairs within the canals and chambers. Sometimes vaselike, sometimes branching, sometimes simply flat shapeless crusts, they occur in a variety of forms and colors. Detailed identification depends on examination of the limy, glassy, or horny spicules that form their skeletons.

COELENTERATE (*Sea Anemone*)

Coelenterata—Hydroids, Jellyfish, Sea Anemones, Corals

Despite their apparent diversity of form, all coelenterates consist basically of a hollow sac closed at one end and surrounded at the other by a ring of tentacles. The characteristic central digestive cavity is called the coelenteron, which means "hollow gut." Another distinctive feature is the possession of stinging cells, unique structures that shoot out poison-filled barbs when touched; stinging cells are used both for defense and for paralyzing prey. In many cases, coelenterate life histories are marked by alternation of generations, with one generation reproducing by budding and the next by sexual means.

COMB JELLY (*Pleurobrachia*)

Ctenophora—Comb Jellies

These simple transparent animals, sometimes known as sea walnuts, once were thought to be coelenterates. However, they lack stinging cells, and their branching digestive cavities are far more complex than the typical coelenterate "hollow gut." Comb jellies differ from all other animals in the possession of comb-plates, eight rows of cilia (hairs) fused together like the teeth on a comb. They swim by rhythmically beating these comb-plates.

Platyhelminthes—Flatworms

Although the best-known examples of flatworms are the parasitic flukes and tapeworms, many free-living species occur in the sea. Some creep among seaweed and on the ocean floor, while others swim by flapping winglike margins of their bodies. The mouth is located more or less centrally on the underside of the flattened, leaflike body. Despite their simplicity, flatworms represent a significant advance over more primitive groups. In addition to greater complexity in their internal structure, they have distinct head ends, right and left sides, and upper and lower surfaces.

FLATWORM (*Bdelloura*)

Nemertea—Ribbon Worms

Varying from only an inch or two to as much as ninety feet in length, ribbon worms burrow in the mud or curl up beneath stones along the ocean shore. Within a muscular sheath at the head end is the ribbon worm's distinctive proboscis, a long, flexible structure sometimes equipped with sharp spines at the tip. Ribbon worms capture prey by shooting out the proboscis and wrapping it around their victims. Some species are noted for their tendency to break into many pieces when handled, each fragment later developing into a new individual.

RIBBON WORM (*Cerebratulus lacteus*)

Annelida—Segmented Worms

This group, characterized by division of the body into distinct ringlike segments, includes sandworms, parchment worms, and earthworms. Many species—often very colorful and attractive—live along the shore and in the ocean. Some, such as lugworms, burrow through sand and mud; others, propelled by paddlelike appendages on each segment, are able to swim freely through the water. Still others, such as trumpet worms and sabellarians, dwell in elaborately constructed tubes.

SEGMENTED WORM (*Nereis virens*)

Mollusca—Chitons, Clams, Snails, Squid

This large and varied group includes chitons, bivalves (clams and kin), gastropods (snails and sea slugs), tusk-shells, and squid and their relatives. Molluscs typically have a large muscular foot and a soft unsegmented body covered by a shell. The shell is secreted by the mantle, a layer of tissue that encloses the body cavity. Elaborate modifications of the basic body plan have resulted in great diversity of form within the group. Snails, for example, have a single spiraled shell, while clams, mussels, and scallops are covered by paired doorlike shells. Sea slugs, in con-

MOLLUSC (*Whelk*)

ARTHROPOD (*Lobster*)

BRYOZOAN (*Membranipora*)

ECHINODERM (*Sea Star*)

159

CHORDATE (*Sea Grapes*)

trast, possess no shell at all as adults. In the octopus, the shell is absent, and the typical muscular foot is divided into eight arms.

Arthropoda—Joint-footed Animals

This largest of all animal groups includes such varied forms as insects, crustaceans, spiders, centipedes, and horseshoe crabs. Arthropods differ from all other animals in the possession of hard protective body coverings and paired jointed legs. The vast majority of marine arthropods are crustaceans—crabs, lobsters, shrimps, and a host of smaller, less familiar forms such as copepods, amphipods, isopods, and barnacles. Because of their abundance in the plankton, where they are the most important primary consumers, many of the smaller crustaceans are the principal food sources for larger marine animals. Several of the larger forms, on the other hand, are prized as human food.

Bryozoa—Moss Animals

Embedded in jellylike material or, more commonly, encased in horny or limy compartments, bryozoans live in colonies of many individuals. Some form delicate lacy crusts on rocks and other surfaces, while others live in upright branching colonies that are often mistaken for seaweeds. Because the mouth of each individual is surrounded by a horseshoe-shaped ridge bearing a row of tentacles, bryozoans once were thought to belong to the hydroid and jellyfish group. Their digestive tracts and other internal features, however, are considerably more complex than those of coelenterates.

Echinodermata—Spiny-skinned Animals

The echinoderms include several seemingly diverse forms—sea stars, sea urchins and sand dollars, brittle stars, sea cucumbers, and sea lilies—yet all are linked by distinctive characteristics. Their bodies are radially symmetrical (wheel-like), with the parts usually occurring in fives. They possess water-vascular systems and hydraulic tube feet. Finally, their skins are stiffened by limy plates, sometimes with spines projecting from the surface. (*Echinodermata* means "hedgehog skin.") All echinoderms live in the sea.

Chordata—Animals with Notochords

All chordates at some stage in their life history possess a stiffened rod (*notochord*) along the back surface. The group includes all the vertebrates (fish, amphibians, reptiles, birds, and mammals), as well as several less-obviously related forms. Most familiar of the primitive chordates are tunicates or sea squirts. Although tunicates possess the characteristic notochord during their tadpolelike larval stage, as adults they generally resemble plump leathery bags topped by a pair of spouts. They live by filtering food from currents of water pumped through their complex bodies. Sea grapes and sea pork are common representatives.

216

Some Common Coastal Fishes

SPINY DOGFISH, 2½ to 3½ feet long, lives in cooler waters throughout the world. Often traveling in large schools, this relatively harmless shark feeds mainly on small fish. Like most other sharks, it bears its young alive.

COMMON ANCHOVY swims in tremendous schools off sandy shores on the Atlantic and Gulf coasts. Silvery three- to four-inch-long anchovies feed on small crustaceans and are eaten in turn by larger fish. Pacific coast relatives are harvested commercially.

COMMON KILLIFISH and many relatives abound in brackish marshes and inlets along all our coasts. Valued for its habit of preying upon mosquito larvae, this remarkably hardy five-inch-long fish thrives even in polluted water.

COMMON SKATE, seldom more than two feet long, lurks on sandy bottoms along the northern Atlantic coast. It feeds on crustaceans and molluscs. Like all sharks, skates, and rays, its skeleton is formed of cartilage rather than bone.

ATLANTIC NEEDLEFISH, occasionally as much as four feet long, lives mostly in southern waters, with a similar species occurring along the California coast. The fragile-looking beak, lined with sharp teeth, is an efficient weapon for snapping up smaller fish.

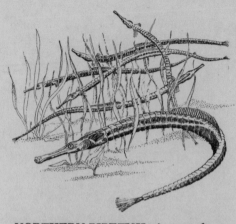

NORTHERN PIPEFISH, six to twelve inches long, is almost invisible as it hovers upright among seaweeds or eelgrass on the mid-Atlantic coast. As with the closely related sea horse, males carry incubating eggs in a brood pouch on the underside.

BLUEFISH, a voracious predator and famed sport fish, travels in great schools along most of the Atlantic coast. Caught both in surf and in deeper water, it averages two to ten pounds; a twenty-five-pounder would win a prize.

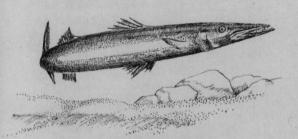

NORTHERN BARRACUDA, a foot-long predator of the mid-Atlantic coast, is a harmless midget compared with the notorious great barracuda of more southern waters. Pacific barracuda, also armed with razor-sharp teeth, is another swift, ferocious hunter.

STRIPED BASS, seldom found far from shore, is a favorite with surfcasters along both coasts. Although it occasionally reaches 125 pounds, ten to fifteen is more common. Since it spawns in bays and rivers, pollution presents a serious hazard in many areas.

ATLANTIC CROAKER gets its name from the peculiar drumming sounds it makes. Especially common in shallows over eelgrass and oyster beds, the foot-long croaker ranges from Cape Cod to Texas, with related species on the West Coast.

PACIFIC SHEEPSHEAD, red in the middle and black on head and tail, is also known as fathead and humpy; the male sports a lump on its forehead during breeding season. This popular game fish of the southern California coast sometimes grows to a length of three feet.

COWFISH, encased in a bony armor of fused scales, is a sluggish swimmer. Common south of the Carolinas, young are sometimes carried far to the north by the Gulf Stream. The tasty foot-long fish occasionally is baked in its own shell.

FOUR-EYED BUTTERFLY FISH, common over Florida coral reefs, occasionally drifts north as far as Cape Cod. Fooled by the large false eyes, predators lunge for its tail while the showy six-inch-long fish darts off unscathed.

SPINY BOXFISH, or burrfish, a ten-inch-long living pincushion, ranges from the West Indies to Cape Cod. When molested, it inflates its body with air or water until it resembles a prickly balloon. Small crustaceans are its favorite foods.

NORTHERN SEA ROBIN uses the hooklike rays beneath its forefins to drag itself across the bottom and probe for crustaceans and other morsels. It croaks noisily during the spawning season.

STRIPED BLENNY, olive-green and four or five inches long, is found from New York to Florida. Members of this widespread family are among the most abundant fish in shallows, tide pools, and brackish inlets throughout the world.

CABEZON, a bizarre scaleless sculpin up to 2½ feet long, lurks in the shallows over rocky bottoms all along the Pacific coast. Many kinds of sculpins, all with armored heads and tapering bodies, live in cold waters along both coasts.

BARRED SEA PERCH never lays eggs; like all the surf perches, it bears its young alive. Sunfish-like and seldom over a foot long, it is a popular game fish of surf and sandy bays all along the West Coast.

KELP GREENLING, also called sea trout, is a popular game fish found from central California to Alaska. About twenty inches long, it feeds on crustaceans and small fish. The gray-brown males are dotted with blue, the females with dark brown.

Adaptation: An inherited characteristic that improves an organism's chances for survival in a particular habitat; may be either structural or functional (physiological). *See also* Mutation.

Alga (plural *algae*): The simplest of all plant forms, having neither roots, stems, nor leaves. Range in size from single cells to branching forms 100 feet or more in length. Larger marine forms are known as *seaweeds*. *See also* Frond; Holdfast.

Alternation of generations: Reproductive pattern in which one generation reproduces sexually, the next by nonsexual means, the next sexually, and so on. *Hydroids* are an outstanding example of this type of life cycle: the sessile hydroid generation produces *medusae* by *budding*, and the medusoid generation reproduces sexually to form individuals that develop into the hydroid generation. Sea lettuce (*Ulva*) is a parallel example in the plant kingdom, reproducing alternately by spores and then by sperms and eggs. *See also* Sexual reproduction.

Amphipods: A group of small crustaceans that have compressed bodies (flattened from side to side) and legs that can be used for both swimming and walking. Beach hoppers are familiar representatives of the group.

Antenna (plural *antennae*): A feeler; an appendage, usually sensory in function, that occurs in pairs on the heads of crustaceans, insects, and other animals.

Appendage: An arm or other limb that branches from an animal's body.

Aristotle's lantern: A name for the sea urchin's specialized mouth parts; an elaborate lanternlike structure composed basically of five large teeth and a system of rods and muscles that move the teeth.

Arthropods: Animals with jointed legs and hard external skeletons. The group includes insects, crustaceans, spiders, and many other types of animals.

Association: A group of plants or animals that characteristically occur together.

Barnacle zone: Zone on a rocky coast where barnacles are the most prominent form of life; usually at or near the middle of the intertidal zone. *See also* Zonation.

Beach wrack: Dead seaweed, animal shells, and other debris deposited at *high-tide mark* as the tide recedes.

Biological clock: An inherited time-measuring process within a living thing; governs its responses to certain external events, such as the rise and fall of the tide or the change from day to night.

Bivalve: Possessing two valves, or shells. Bivalve molluscs include oysters, clams, and similar animals.

Bloom: *See* Plankton bloom.

Bryozoans: "Moss-animals"; a group of minute animals that live in colonies of many individuals, each dwelling in a fleshy, horny, or limy cell or compartment. Some species form branching plantlike colonies that are often mistaken for seaweeds, while others form delicate limy crusts on stones or other surfaces.

Budding: A nonsexual method of reproduction in which part of an animal's body separates from the parent and develops into an independent adult. *See also* Sexual reproduction.

Carapace: A hard shell-like covering on the

upper side of an animal's body, such as the upper shell of a crab or a turtle.

Carnivorous: Meat-eating; descriptive of organisms that feed on the flesh of animals.

Chlorophyll: A group of pigments that produces the green color of plants; essential to *photosynthesis*.

Chordate: An animal with a nerve cord running along its back and a stiffened rod just beneath the nerve cord. The group includes tunicates, lancelets, and all animals with backbones (the *vertebrates*).

Cleaning shrimp: A type of shrimp that lives by feeding on parasites and dead or diseased tissue on the skin of fishes, anemones, or other animals.

Climax: The final or mature association in a natural *succession*; remains relatively stable unless the environment changes drastically.

Coccolithophore: A type of minute single-cell yellow alga found only in the oceans. They are so small that they usually pass through a fine plankton net.

Commensal: An organism that benefits by living in association with another living thing, but whose presence is neither beneficial nor harmful to its host. *See also* Parasite.

Community: All the plants and animals in a particular habitat that are bound together by *food chains* and other interrelations.

Competition: The struggle between individuals or groups of living things for common necessities, such as food or living space.

Continental shelf: The bottom of the relatively shallow seas fringing a continent; ends where the bottom drops off abruptly to the great depths of the abyss. The shelf may vary from a few miles to one hundred or more in width.

Copepods: A group of minute crustaceans that have rounded bodies and oarlike swimming antennae. Many species of copepods occur in the plankton, often in immense numbers.

Crustacean: A member of the large group of animals that includes lobsters, crabs, barnacles, amphipods, copepods, and similar forms. Crustaceans are characterized by jointed legs, segmented bodies, and a hard external skeleton.

Current: A mass of water circulating along a more or less definite route in the ocean. The major currents flow in great circular patterns around the oceans, clockwise in the Northern Hemisphere, counterclockwise in the Southern Hemisphere.

Detritus: Minute particles of the decaying remains of dead plants and animals; an important source of food for many marine animals.

Diatom: A single-cell alga encased in an intricately etched silica shell formed of two halves that fit together like the lid on a box. Because of their abundance in the *plankton*, diatoms are the most important *primary producers* in the sea.

Dinoflagellates: A group of single-cell organisms that possess characteristics of both plants and animals. Like plants, dinoflagellates can manufacture food through *photosynthesis*; they can also move about like animals.

Diurnal: Active during daylight hours.

Echinoderm: "Spiny-skinned animal," a group that includes sea stars, sea urchins, sand dollars, sea cucumbers, and other marine animals; characterized by hard plates or spines under the skin, five-part *radial symmetry*, and a water-vascular system, among other features.

Ecological niche: An organism's role in a natural community, such as *scavenger* or *primary producer* of food. Refers to function, not the place where it is found.

Ecological types: Organisms that fill the same general role (*niche*) in a community, need not be closely related since similarity is in function, not ancestry. For example, in different habitats or at different times of day in the same habitat, entirely unrelated species may function as *scavengers*.

Ecology: The scientific study of the relationships of living things to one another and to their environment. A scientist who studies these relationships is an ecologist.

Ecotone: An area of transition from one type of habitat to another, such as a zone where muddy and sandy areas merge along a beach. The region with characteristics of both habitats usually supports denser, more varied populations of plants and animals than does either one by itself; this tendency is known as the "edge effect."

Ectocrine: An "environmental hormone"; a chemical secretion released by a living thing into its environment, where it stimulates specific responses in other individuals.

Edge effect: *See* Ecotone.

Egg: Female reproductive cell. *See also* Sexual reproduction; Fertilization.

Embryo: A developing individual before its birth or hatching.

Environment: All the external conditions surrounding a living thing.

Estuary: A tidal river; portion of a river that is affected by rise and fall of the tide and that contains a graded mixture of fresh and salt water.

Fertilization: The union of a male reproductive cell (*sperm*) with a female reproductive cell (*egg*); essential step in *sexual reproduction*.

Filter-feeder: An animal equipped with elaborate sieves, tentacles, filters, or other devices for straining *plankton* and minute particles of *detritus* from sea water.

Flagellum (plural *flagella*): A whiplike structure used for locomotion by many single-cell organisms, such as dinoflagellates.

Food chain: A series of plants and animals linked by their food relationships. *Plankton,* a plankton-eating fish, and a fish-eating bird would form a simple food chain. Any one species is usually represented in many food chains. *See also* Food web.

Food web: An interlocking system of *food chains.* Since few animals rely on a single source of food and because no food source is consumed by only one species of animal, the separate food chains in every natural community interlock and form a food web.

Fragmentation: The development of new individuals from pieces broken from the body of the parent.

Frond: The leaflike body of an alga.

Fucoid alga: *Rockweed*-type alga.

Groin: A type of sea wall that projects from the shore; designed to control the movement of sand by *longshore currents.* Groins are usually built in series along a coast.

Grunion: A small edible fish found along the coast of southern California; noted for its remarkable spawning behavior.

Habitat: The immediate surroundings (living place) of a plant or animal.

High-tide mark: The uppermost level on a shoreline to be reached by the highest tides.

Holdfast: The rootlike base of a marine alga. Anchors the plant to rocks or other surfaces, but has no specific adaptations for absorbing water or nutrients.

Hormone: A chemical substance produced internally by a living thing; regulates the functioning of another part of its body.

Hydroid: An animal of the jellyfish group, with an upright tubular body surmounted by a ring of tentacles surrounding the mouth. Often grow in plantlike branching colonies with different individuals specialized for various functions, as feeding or reproduction.

Intertidal zone: The area along a coastline which is alternately covered by water and exposed to air because of the rise and fall of tides; the area between *high-tide mark* and *low-tide mark*. Sometimes subdivided into upper and lower intertidal zones because of differences in their daily periods of submergence. *See also* Zonation.

Invertebrate: An animal without a backbone. Generally the nerve cord runs close to the under (ventral) surface of its body. *See also* Vertebrate.

Isopods: A group of small crustaceans that have flattened bodies (top to bottom) and many legs of more or less equal size; most species are scavengers.

Kelp: Large, straplike brown alga with strong *holdfasts*, found mostly in cooler waters. Various species range from the lower *intertidal zone* to waters a hundred feet or more deep.

Laminarian: *Kelp*-type alga.

Larva (plural *larvae*): An immature animal whose form differs from the adult form, such as the planktonic swimming stage in the development of a barnacle.

Longshore current: An ocean current that flows parallel to a coastline; results from waves striking the shore at an angle.

Low-tide mark: The lowest level of a shoreline to be exposed during ebb tide.

Marine biology: A field of science concerned especially with the study of living things in the sea.

Medusa (plural *medusae*): Jellyfish, a simple umbrella-shaped animal with a ring of *stinging tentacles* trailing from its margin. Some medusae represent the free-swimming sexual generation of *hydroids*, whose life histories are marked by *alternation of generations.*

Megalops: A late larval stage in the development of certain crustaceans; resembles the adult more closely than does the earlier *zoea* stage.

Metabolism: The sum of the chemical activities taking place in the cells of a living thing.

Metamorphosis: A change in the form of a living thing as it matures, especially the transformation from a *larva* to an adult.

Molt: To shed a body covering, such as the shell-like external skeleton of a crustacean.

Moss-animal: *See* Bryozoan.

Mutation: A sudden change in the make-up of an organism's germ cells, resulting in offspring that possess characteristics markedly different from those of either parent. Mutations generally are harmful but occasionally may improve an organism's chances for survival. *See also* Adaptation.

Mysid: A minute shrimplike crustacean that often occurs in great numbers in the plankton.

Nocturnal: Active at night.

Nudibranch: Sea slug; a marine snail that possesses no shell as an adult. The backs of many species are covered by fingerlike projections that function as gills.

Oceanography: The scientific study of the sea in all its aspects—physical, chemical, and biological.

Oyster coral: The common name for twisted masses of limy tubes sometimes found on oyster shells; the tubes are built by tubeworms, not coral animals.

Oyster hand: A group of oysters cemented into a cluster.

Oyster cracker: Toadfish, a species of fish commonly associated with oyster beds.

Parasite: A plant or animal that lives in or on another living thing (its host) and obtains part or all of its food from the host's body. *See also* Commensal.

Periwinkle: Small marine snail. Many species occur on rocky coasts throughout most of the world.

Pesticide: A substance, usually chemical, employed to kill organisms that man considers undesirable.

Photosynthesis: The process by which green plants convert carbon dioxide and water into simple sugar. *Chlorophyll* and sunlight are essential to the series of complex chemical reactions involved.

Phytoplankton: Plant *plankton*.

Plankton: The minute plants and animals that float or swim near the surface of a body of water. The enormous quantities of plant plankton (*phytoplankton*) and animal plankton (*zooplankton*) in sea water provide an important food source for many animals.

Plankton bloom: An explosive increase in the plankton population on an area of the ocean's surface. Results from a sudden improvement in growing conditions, such as an increase in available nutrients. Numbers may become so great as to color the surface of the water visibly.

Plankton tow: A method of collecting minute planktonic plants and animals by pulling a fine-mesh plankton net through the water, usually behind a boat.

Pollution: The fouling of water resources with sewage, industrial wastes, and other contaminants, making them unfit to support many forms of life.

Polyp: An individual member of a *hydroid* colony.

Predator: An animal that lives by capturing other animals for food.

Primary consumer: A plant-eating animal; an animal that converts the primary production of plants into animal tissue. *See also* Primary producers; Secondary consumer.

Primary producers: Plants, the basic link in any *food chain*; by means of *photosynthesis*, plants manufacture the food on which all other living things ultimately depend. *See also* Primary consumer.

Production pyramid: The diminishing amount of organic material produced at each successive level along a *food chain*. The declining productivity results from the constant loss of energy through metabolism along the food chain. *See also* Pyramid of numbers.

Protozoan: A simple one-cell animal such as *Amoeba* or *Paramecium*.

Pyramid of numbers: The normally declining number of individuals at each successive level on a *food chain*. For example, a given number of plants will ultimately support fewer higher-order consumers than first-order consumers. *See also* Production pyramid.

Radial symmetry: Wheel-like body organization, with all parts radiating from a common center.

Radula: A tonguelike structure covered with minute horny protuberances similar to the teeth on a file. Found in snails and certain other molluscs; used for rasping food from rocks or for boring through the shells of other animals.

Regeneration: The process of replacing lost body parts, as when a sea star grows a new arm where one has broken off.

Rip current: A turbulent current flowing away from the shore, as in an area where a river flows into the sea.

Rockweed: Brownish-green alga with air bladders and flattened branching *fronds*. Many species occur in the *intertidal zone* on cool rocky coasts.

Scavenger: An animal that eats the dead remains and wastes of other animals and plants. *See also* Predator.

Sea slug: *See* Nudibranch.

Seaweed: Any large marine alga, such as sea lettuce or kelp.

Secondary consumer: An animal that feeds on plant-eaters. Plants (*primary producers*), plant-eaters (*primary consumers*), and *predators* (secondary consumers) would form three links in a *food chain*. *See also* Third-order consumer.

Sessile: Permanently attached to a surface.

Sexual reproduction: Formation of a new generation through the union of male and female germ cells.

Spat: Immature oysters newly settled upon an available surface.

Spawn: To shed reproductive cells; refers to animals such as fish and crustaceans that shed eggs and sperm directly into the water.

Sperm: Male reproductivè cell. *See also* Fertilization; Sexual reproduction.

Splash zone: Area above *high-tide mark* on a rocky coast which is moistened by spray from waves breaking on the rocks below. *See also* Zonation.

Stinging cell: A specialized structure found in jellyfish and their relatives, consisting of a sharply pointed, poison-filled thread coiled within a capsule in the animal's skin. The poisonous thread is released on contact and serves both as a defense mechanism and as an aid in capturing prey.

Stinging tentacle: A tentacle armed with *stinging cells.*

Subtidal zone: The area of a beach that lies below the level of low tide. *See also* Zonation.

Succession: The gradual replacement of one community by another, leading eventually to a more or less stable *climax* community.

Third-order consumer: A *predator* that feeds on *secondary consumers.*

226

Tide: The periodic rise and fall of the waters of the ocean, resulting from the gravitational attraction of the moon and, to a lesser extent, the sun. A complete cycle of rise and fall requires approximately twelve hours and twenty-five minutes for completion.

Tide pool: A pool of sea water temporarily isolated in the *intertidal* region as a result of the ebbing of the tide.

Tube feet: Specialized sucking feet operated by hydraulic pressure; found in sea stars and their relatives. *See also* Water-vascular system.

Types: *See* Ecological types.

Upper beach: The area of a beach that lies above *high-tide mark. See also* Zonation.

Valves: Movable doorlike structures, such as the two halves of a clam shell or the pair of movable plates at the top of a barnacle's shell.

Vertebrate: An animal with a backbone. The group includes fishes, amphibians, reptiles, birds, and mammals.

Water-vascular system: A system of canals, bulbs, and *tube feet* filled with water; found in sea stars and their relatives. The system functions in controlling operation of the tube feet.

Wave: A form of energy that travels through a medium in the form of a progressive disturbance, but does not cause particles of the medium to advance with it.

Zoea: An early, free-swimming larval stage in the development of many crustaceans. *See also* Megalops.

Zonation: Organization of a habitat into more or less parallel bands of distinctive plant and animal associations as a result of variations in environmental conditions. Zones along the shore include the *upper beach* (sandy shore) or *splash zone* (rocky shore), the *intertidal zone,* and the *subtidal zone.*

Zooplankton: Animal *plankton.*

Bibliography

ANIMALS

ABBOTT, R. TUCKER. *American Seashells*. Van Nostrand, 1954.

BREDER, CHARLES M., JR. *Field Book of Marine Fishes of the Atlantic Coast*. Putnam, 1948.

BUCHSBAUM, RALPH. *Animals without Backbones*. University of Chicago Press, 1948.

BUCHSBAUM, RALPH, and LORUS J. MILNE. *The Lower Animals*. Doubleday, 1961.

CURTIS, BRIAN. *The Life Story of the Fish*. Dover, 1949.

GALTSOFF, PAUL S. *The American Oyster*. Fisheries Bulletin No. 64, U.S. Government Printing Office, 1964.

HEDGPETH, JOEL W. *Introduction to Seashore Life of the San Francisco Bay Region and the Coast of Northern California*. University of California Press, 1962.

LIGHT, SOL F., and others. *Intertidal Invertebrates of the Central California Coast*. University of California Press, 1957.

MACGINITIE, GEORGE E., and NETTIE MACGINITIE. *Natural History of Marine Animals*. McGraw-Hill, 1949.

MINER, ROY WALDO. *Field Book of Seashore Life*. Putnam, 1950.

MORRIS, PERCY A. *A Field Guide to the Shells of Our Atlantic and Gulf Coasts*. Houghton Mifflin, 1951.

MORRIS, PERCY A. *A Field Guide to the Shells of the Pacific Coast and Hawaii*. Houghton Mifflin, 1952.

NICOL, J. A. C. *The Biology of Marine Animals*. Interscience, 1960.

PETERSON, ROGER TORY. *A Field Guide to the Birds*. Houghton Mifflin, 1947.

PETERSON, ROGER TORY. *A Field Guide to Western Birds*. Houghton Mifflin, 1961.

SMITH, RALPH I. (Editor). *Keys to Marine Invertebrates of the Woods Hole Region*. Marine Biological Laboratory, 1964.

ZIM, HERBERT S., and HURST H. SHOEMAKER. *Fishes*. Golden Press, 1957.

PLANKTON

DAVIS, CHARLES C. *The Marine and Fresh-water Plankton*. Michigan State University Press, 1955.

HARDY, ALISTER C. *The Open Sea*. Houghton Mifflin, 1956.

PLANTS

DICKINSON, C. I. *British Seaweeds*. Eyre and Spottiswoode (London), 1963.

SMITH, GILBERT M. *Marine Algae of the Monterey Peninsula, California*. Stanford University Press, 1944.

TAYLOR, WILLIAM R. *Marine Algae of the Northeastern Coast of North America*. University of Michigan Press, 1957.

MARINE BIOLOGY

BURTON, MAURICE. *Margins of the Sea*. Harper, 1954.

EVANS, I. O. (Editor). *Sea and Seashore*. Warne, 1962.

JÄGERSTEN, GÖSTA. *Life in the Sea*. Basic Books, 1964.

LE DANOIS, E. *Marine Life of Coastal Waters*. Harrap (London), 1957.

MARSHALL, N. B. *Aspects of Deep Sea Biology*. Philosophical Library, 1954.

RICKETTS, EDWARD F., and JACK CALVIN. *Between Pacific Tides*. Stanford University Press, 1962.

YONGE, C. M. *The Sea Shore*. Collins (London), 1949.

ZIM, HERBERT S., and LESTER INGLE. *Seashores*. Golden Press, 1955.

ECOLOGY

ALLEE, WARDER C., and others. *Principles of Animal Ecology*. Saunders, 1949.

ANDREWARTHA, H. G. *Introduction to the Study of Animal Populations*. University of Chicago Press, 1961.

BUCHSBAUM, RALPH, and MILDRED BUCHSBAUM. *Basic Ecology*. Boxwood Press, 1957.

FARB, PETER, and THE EDITORS OF LIFE. *Ecology*. Time, Inc., 1963.

LEWIS, J. R. *The Ecology of Rocky Shores*. English Universities Press, 1964.

MOORE, HILARY B. *Marine Ecology*. Wiley, 1958.

ODUM, EUGENE P., and HOWARD T. ODUM. *Fundamentals of Ecology*. Saunders, 1959.

REID, GEORGE K. *Ecology of Inland Waters and Estuaries*. Reinhold, 1961.

OCEANOGRAPHY

BASCOM, WILLARD. *Waves and Beaches*. Doubleday, 1964.

COKER, R. E. *This Great and Wide Sea*. University of North Carolina Press, 1947.

COWEN, ROBERT C. *Frontiers of the Sea*. Doubleday, 1963.

DEFANT, ALBERT. *Ebb and Flow*. University of Michigan Press, 1958.

RUSSELL, FREDERICK S., and C. M. YONGE. *The Seas*. Warne, 1963.

STOMMEL, HENRY. *The Gulf Stream*. University of California Press, 1958.

SVERDRUP, H. U., MARTIN W. JOHNSON, and RICHARD H. FLEMING. *The Oceans*. Prentice-Hall, 1942.

GENERAL READING

BATES, MARSTON. *The Forest and the Sea*. Random House, 1960.

BERRILL, N. J. *The Living Tide*. Dodd, Mead, 1951.

BESTON, HENRY. *The Outermost House*. Rinehart, 1949.

BUTCHER, DEVEREUX. *Exploring Our National Parks and Monuments*. Houghton Mifflin, 1960.

BUTCHER, DEVEREUX. *Exploring Our National Wild Life Refuges*. Houghton Mifflin, 1963.

CARSON, RACHEL. *The Edge of the Sea*. Houghton Mifflin, 1955.

CARSON, RACHEL. *The Sea Around Us*. Oxford University Press, 1961.

ENGEL, LEONARD, and THE EDITORS OF LIFE. *The Sea*. Time, Inc., 1961.

RICHARDSON, WYMAN. *The House on Nauset Marsh*. Norton, 1955.

Illustration Credits and Acknowledgments

COVER: Sandpiper, Jerry Cooke from Photo Researchers.

UNCAPTIONED PHOTOGRAPHS: 8–9: Martha's Vineyard, Massachusetts, William H. Amos 64–65: Big Sur, California, William Garnett 136–137: Local invertebrates, Woods Hole, Massachusetts, George Lower 176–177: Cape Hatteras National Seashore, North Carolina, Peter G. Sanchez

ALL OTHER ILLUSTRATIONS: 10: Bucky Reeves from National Audubon Society 11: R. W. Carpenter 12: Felix Cooper 13: William Garnett 14: Peter Sanchez; Ruth Kirk 15: Patricia Henrichs 16: George Lower 17: Les D. Line 18–19: Peter Sanchez 20: Patricia Henrichs 21–22: William H. Amos 23: Patricia Henrichs 24–26: William H. Amos 27: Ruth Kirk 28–29: C. Newman 30: Felix Cooper 31: Moody Institute of Science 32: Dr. Charles J. Stine; William H. Amos 33: Dr. Alexander B. Klots 34: William H. Amos 35: Graphic Arts International 36–37: Dr. Charles J. Stine 38: Patricia Henrichs 39: Jack Dermid 40: George Lower 42–43: Felix Cooper 44: William Garnett 45: Patricia Henrichs 46: Felix Cooper 47: Joseph Muench 48: K. B. Clarke from Black Star 49: Harry L. Beede 50–51: Ruth Kirk 52–54: William H. Amos 55: Graphic Arts International 56: Joseph Muench 57: Robert Strindberg 58: Hugh M. Halliday from National Audubon Society 59: Felix Cooper 61: Laurence Lowry from Rapho-Guillumette 62–63: Roy Latham 66–67: Charles Fracé 68–69: William H. Amos 70: Sonja Bullaty from National Audubon Society 71: Jack Dermid 72: Ansel Adams 73: Robert Strindberg 74–75: Charles Fracé 76: Lynwood Chace 77: National Park Service Photo 78: Robert C. Hermes 79–80: William H. Amos 81: Patricia Henrichs 82–83: Verna R. Johnston 84–85: William H. Amos 86: Graphic Arts International 87: Charles Fracé 88–89: Ansel Adams 90: William H. Amos; Barbara Taylor 91–92: William H. Amos 93: Walter Dawn 94: Ralph Anderson, National Park Service Photo 95: National Park Service Photo 96–99: William H. Amos 100: Grambs Miller 101–103: William H. Amos 104: Ruth Kirk 105: Peter Sanchez 106: William H. Amos 107–108: Ruth Kirk 109: William H. Amos 110: Donald Heintzelman 111: Bucky Reeves 112–115: William H. Amos 116–117: Douglas Faulkner 118–119: Woodbridge Williams, National Park Service Photo 120–121: Charles Fracé 122: Leonard Lee Rue from National Audubon Society 123: John Gerard from National Audubon Society; Donald Heintzelman from National Audubon Society; Leonard Lee Rue from National Audubon Society 124: William H. Amos 125: Graphic Arts International 126–128: William H. Amos 129: Felix Cooper 130: Charles Fracé 131: American Museum of Natural History 132–133: James A. Kern 134: Bob and Ira Spring 138: Graphic Arts International from C. L. Newcombe and R. W. Menzel, 1945, Contribution No. 22, Virginia Fisheries Laboratory 139: Woodbridge Williams 140–141: Patricia Henrichs 142: Betty Barford; Melbourne R. Carriker 143: William H. Amos; Patricia Henrichs 144–150: William H. Amos 151: Patricia Henrichs 152–155: William H. Amos 155: Felix Cooper 156: Bucky Reeves 157: Ruth Kirk 158: Ruth Kirk 159: William H. Amos: Ruth Kirk 160: Robert Strindberg 161: Patricia Henrichs 162: Felix Cooper 163: William H. Amos 164: Felix Cooper 165: William H. Amos 166–167: James A. Kern 168: Russ Kinne from Photo Researchers; Felix Cooper 169: William H. Amos 170: Woodbridge Williams 171: Felix Cooper 172–173: Charles Fracé 174: Tom Hollyman from Photo Researchers 178: Grambs Miller 179: William H. Amos 180: Dennis Brokaw from National Audubon Society 181: Walter Dawn 182–183: Walter Dawn 184–185: Allan D. Cruickshank from National Audubon Society 186–188: Graphic Arts International 189: Woodbridge Williams 190: Bruce Roberts from Rapho-Guillumette, courtesy of *International Harvester World* 192: Betty Barford 193: Joseph Muench 194: Melbourne R. Carriker 195: Everglades Natural History Association 196: William Bolte 197: Everglades Natural History Association 198: William Garnett 201–205: Charles Fracé 206–207: Graphic Arts International 208–216: Charles Fracé 217–220: Patricia Henrichs 232: Charles Fracé

PHOTO EDITOR: ROBERT J. WOODWARD

AUTHOR'S ACKNOWLEDGMENTS: *A book of this sort is a compendium of knowledge from a great many sources, and my debts to others are far too numerous and too detailed to mention here. I wish to acknowledge, however, a long-term exchange of ideas with colleagues at the University of Delaware Marine Laboratory, in particular Drs. Franklin C. Daiber, Carl N. Shuster, and Charles M. Wilber, and with colleagues at the Systematics-Ecology Program, Marine Biological Laboratory, Woods Hole, especially Drs. Melbourne R. Carriker, Edwin T. Moul, and Victor Zullo, and Messrs. J. Stewart Nagle and Peter J. Oldham. My students over many years have tested much of what this book contains, and their suggestions and discoveries have helped to shape the ideas presented here. My greatest debt of gratitude is to my wife Catherine, whose care and critical eye have had a profound effect upon this book, and who has shared with me work in both the field and the laboratory.*

(The publisher also wishes to thank Wayne W. Bryant, William Perry, and M. Woodbridge Williams of the National Park Service for their assistance in reading the manuscript and locating photographs.)

228

Index

[Page numbers in boldface type indicate reference to illustrations.]

231